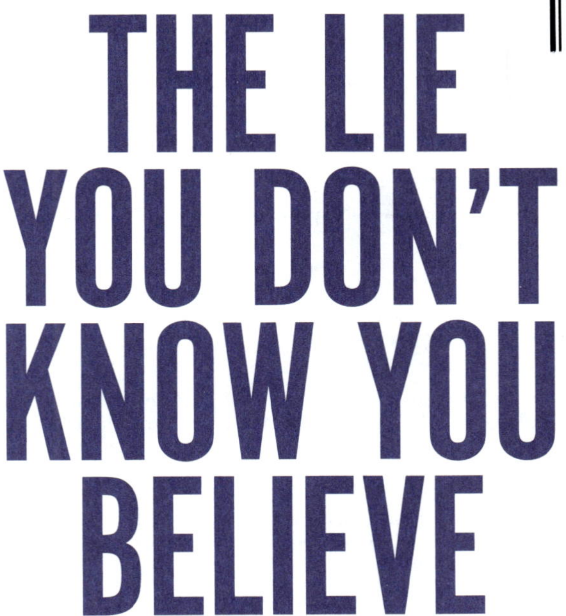

HOW JESUS FOUGHT THE DEVIL IN THE BOOK OF MATTHEW

A SIX-SESSION BIBLE STUDY

JENNIE ALLEN

The Lie You Don't Know You Believe Bible Study Guide

Published by HarperChristian Resources, 3950 Sparks Drive SE, Suite 101, Grand Rapids, MI 49546, USA. HarperChristian Resources is a registered trademark of HarperCollins Christian Publishing, Inc.

Requests for information should be addressed to customercare@harpercollins.com.

ISBN 978-0-310-17041-9 (softcover)

ISBN 978-0-310-17042-6 (ebook)

HarperChristian Resources titles may be purchased in bulk for church, business, fundraising, or ministry use. For information, please email ResourceSpecialist@ChurchSource.com.

HarperCollins Publishers, Macken House, 39/40 Mayor Street Upper, Dublin 1, D01 C9W8, Ireland (https://www.harpercollins.com).

Art Direction: Ron Huizinga
Cover Design: Marshall Creative
Interior Design: Thinkpen Design

First Printing January 2026 / Printed in the United States of America

CONTENTS

What do you hope to get out of this study?

____

____

____

____

____

GET HONEST

This may be a little confrontational, and possibly uncomfortable, but it will be worth it. We will be dealing with tender moments from childhood, calling up some beliefs about ourselves that may have lain dormant for a long time, and confronting lies with truth. But God has brought you here for a reason. He intends for you to live in truth and freedom. Until we start living in His kingdom, we will miss the real, rich experience of life He intends for us. If you feel depleted, limited, and not entirely yourself, are you also willing to consider that you may have been believing a lie? Even if it takes some time and effort to confront those lies and adopt a different perspective? Be compassionate with yourself and get honest with God. He knows all of it already, anyway.

ENGAGE WITH YOUR SMALL GROUP

An important part of moving from lies to truth is a willingness to do it with the help of others. I know it can be scary, but I'm going to ask you to be vulnerable and acknowledge the connection developing with those who are vulnerable with you too. Try to listen and speak without judgment. Keep your group a safe and confidential place to wrestle and discover. A place filled with truth. John describes Christ as being "full of grace and truth" (John 1:14). I pray that this is how your small group will be described.

"'And you shall know the truth, and the truth shall make you free'" (John 8:32 NKJV).

COMMIT TO BEING CONSISTENT AND PRESENT

Every time you gather with your group you will be building new skills for living healthfully with your emotions and learning how God feels. Consistency and presence show respect to God and those around you in this process. Arrange your schedule so you don't miss any part of this journey. Have your projects finished when you come to the group meeting (except the first one, which we'll do together).

"Everyone should be quick to listen, slow to speak and slow to become angry" (James 1:19 NIV).

GROUND RULES FOR GROUP DISCUSSION TIME

BE CONCISE.

Share your answers to the questions while protecting others' time for sharing. Be thoughtful, and try to respond to "I feel" statements with another "I feel" statement. *Do not judge or condemn other people's feelings.* Don't be afraid to share with the group, but try not to dominate the conversation.

KEEP GROUP MEMBERS' STORIES CONFIDENTIAL.

Many things your group members share are things they choose to share with you, not with your husband or other friends. Protect each other by not allowing anything shared in the group to leave the group.

RELY ON SCRIPTURE FOR TRUTH.

We are prone to use conventional, worldly wisdom as truth. While there is value in that, this is not the place. If you feel led to respond, please only respond with God's Truth and Word, not "advice."

NO COUNSELING.

Protect the group by not directing all attention toward solving one person's problem. This is the place for confession and discovery and applying truth together as a group. Your group leader will be able to direct you to more help outside the group time if you need it. Don't be afraid to ask for help.

STUDY DESIGN

In the first meeting, your group's study guides will be passed out, and you will work through Session 1 together. After that, each session in the study guide is meant to be completed on your own during the week before coming to the group meeting. Each week begins with a short intro before moving into the portion marked Study. The Study portion is followed by four application Projects to allow God to further change your heart and life, then closing thoughts from me. The Study and Projects can be completed in one sitting or broken up into smaller parts throughout the week depending on your needs.

These lessons may feel very different from studies you have done in the past. They are very interactive. The beginning of each lesson will involve you, your Bible, and a pen. Work through the Scripture and listen to God's voice. Hear from Him. Allow God to further change your heart and life.

WHAT *THE LIE YOU DON'T KNOW YOU BELIEVE* IS NOT

We all are products of messed-up environments. Even with the best parents, spouses, and friends, we still have emotional wounds, and we all have believed lies about ourselves during painful relational moments, often very early on in life. The hurt and beliefs gained in these relationships take work to process, and there are many great resources your group leader can suggest that take you deeper into the wounds from your past. I believe in the wisdom of Christian counseling from a certified therapist, and there is a time and a place for it. Christian counseling is a process I've gone through many times myself, as have many of my loved ones—it truly brought us so much freedom.

This study might feature some of the same self-reflective elements as counseling, but honestly, it's not intended to be a substitute. If you feel counseling may benefit you through this process, I encourage you to give yourself a gift: Speak to your doctor and look into a therapist for yourself.

"He heals the brokenhearted and binds up their wounds" (Psalm 147:3).

If there was a core lie sabotaging your life, wouldn't you want to know what it is? As you walk through *The Lie You Don't Know You Believe*, my hope is that you'll spot the lie sneaking into your life, trace the moment it took root, and see how the enemy has been using it to keep you stuck. This isn't about behavior modification. This is about transferring your life out of the enemy's kingdom of lies and into the Kingdom of Light—where joy, peace, and strength aren't fleeting feelings but your everyday reality. And as you do, remember: You're not behind; you're not too broken—**you're exactly where freedom begins.**

SESSION 1

IDENTIFY

Pages 10–23 are intended for you to get acclimated to this study on your own before you meet as a group, or together before you watch the first video. Flip to page 24 for Video Teaching.

Have you ever been sick with a mystery ailment no one could explain? You felt it inside, but no one knew what it was. You got so frustrated thinking it all might be in your head. But once you finally discovered what it was, you immediately felt better. You were still sick. You still suffered from the same symptoms. You still felt crummy and weak. But something about naming the problem helped you cope with it a little better. Naming means knowing. It means knowing what you're up against.

That's how I remember feeling as soon as I discovered I was fundamentally believing a lie about myself. I was laboring under ideas about my worth that just weren't true. Sure, I was frustrated to learn I'd been believing that lie. But what I felt most was relief. Relief that my suffering had an origin. Relief that I could know what that origin was. Relief that, by the power of God, I could go back to that origin and find my way forward in health. Relief that, in the same way someone who suffers from cancer is not the cancer, I was not that lie.

That's the kind of relief I want to invite you into. If you're feeling a little sick, a little weak in your soul, you can identify the lie and be healed.

At some level, I believe we're all believing some kind of lie about ourselves. It might not be an in-your-face lie. Your life might look healthy on the surface, but a lie could show up in a vague hopelessness at the end of the day: *There's too much going on. I'm helpless.* In second-guessing that won't stop: *I don't measure up.* In the way you brace for things to go wrong, even when they don't: *No one's here for me.* Maybe you can't put your finger on it, this sense that something's not right. But you've felt its subtle pull. You've felt the devastation, the aloneness of being far from God, far from yourself. And you've tried to convince yourself that everything's normal.

It's not.

It's possible you wouldn't call the lie you believe a "lie," per se. It doesn't feel like a lie. It feels like fact. Like "just who I am." Like the water you're floating in.

But what if it *isn't* who you are? What if one key idea that's been directing your life—quietly, daily—isn't truth at all?

If there was one core lie that was sabotaging your life, wouldn't you want to know it? And wouldn't you want to be free of it?

You *can* be.

Friends, I've seen subtle lies show up in my life for far too long. I've been working and researching and fighting for ways to kick these lies to the curb. For myself, and for those I love. Because when I hear those lies actually slip out of their mouths, I find myself in disbelief. Lies like: *I'm worthless. I'm hopeless. I'm helpless.*

"What?! Are you serious?" I'd say to that. "You're amazing! You have so much hope and so much help!" But the thing about lies is, they don't feel absurd when we don't say them out loud—when they're washing around inside our heads, directing our lives. They don't sound so crazy. They just feel like the way things are. And that's the spell I want to break today.

We have to see how insidious this is. It's like we bob up and down in these untruths day after day, having no clue just how powerfully they're deciding our direction, how devastating they can be. Then, without our realizing it, the lies pull us under. It's slow, and it's quiet. We lose our footing, and we even start believing the riptide is who we are. That somehow, *we* caused it. We're embarrassed about some lie we've believed. We think we deserve to drown for getting caught in it. We flounder, get desperate, and forget that there's a way out.

But there is.

We are *not* caught forever.

We are *not* by ourselves.

We are *not* the lie, and the lie is *not* us.

We are *not* crazy.

We can point and look and *name* what's really going on. We can see the pull of that current for what it truly is. And we can remember and start swimming sideways, fighting our way out of its pull, and reaching for the hand that pulls us out.

Yes, this takes a fight. It is a swim for your life, and for the lives of those you love. We're going to have to work up a little rage—saying, "I'm not going down this way." We're going to have to hate that riptide. Because here's the thing: *It* hates *us*.

THE PROBLEM: THE ENEMY COMES AT US WITH LIES

Here's the bottom line: We have a God who loves us. We also have an enemy who hates us. And the way he gets to us is through lies. Jesus said of our enemy:

> "'The thief comes only to steal and kill and destroy'" (John 10:10).

His number one strategy, it seems, is filling our heads with lies. About ourselves, about God, about the nature of reality. The enemy wants to separate us from God and suck us out to sea.

How does he do this? Any way he can. Lies can reach us through others, ourselves, our childhoods—and we're going to talk about that. Over the next six weeks, we're going to bravely examine what those lies are and where they might have come from. We're going to hold on to the truths that neutralize those lies. But what matters now is realizing that we are existing in them—believing them, subtly in the background. That a master manipulator is leveraging them. But hope comes when we start to see the current around us, pulling us away from the full, healthy life we want to live—a life of confidence and closeness with the God we're created to live with.

So right now, today, I want to draw a line in the sand. *This* is where we stop being clueless about what's going on. *This* is where we acknowledge that someone is actively distorting our perception of ourselves, sowing seeds of doubt about the goodness of God. And together, we will expose him.

WHAT IT LOOKS LIKE TO IDENTIFY THE LIES

So, I'll go first. I'm going to share more about this later, but through prayer and a lot of guided reflection, I spotted my big lie.

Ever since I was about twelve, I've had a nagging fear that I was invisible. That no one noticed me. There had to be a reason for that, right?

I tried to work hard, to achieve, to be pleasing, to get that "well done." All to conceal the background thought that under it all, I wasn't worth anyone's time at all. I was nothing special. My lie that I thought was truth: *I'm worthless.*

And the weird thing was, this felt . . . obvious. Like facts. And there was evidence. It kept popping up. When something good happened, I'd think: *Oh, no, I don't deserve this. This is a fluke.* When I was overlooked or disregarded, I'd think, *Yeah. That tracks.* It wasn't a conscious choice. It was the fabric of how I thought. The backdrop of my inner world.

Lies like this don't even feel like lies anymore. They feel like the truest thing about you. The thing you're trying to manage.

So, what about you? Let me share what some of the women in my community responded with when I asked what dark belief about themselves they're trying to manage:

- *I have to do things myself. No one shows up for me.*
- *No one wants me here.*
- *I deserve every bad thing that happens.*
- *I'm unqualified.*
- *I'm not good enough to have friends.*
- *I'm too much.*
- *I'm not enough.*

Our lies might all look a little different, but, in the end, they all do the same things. They shape the choices we make. They keep us silent, our eyes looking down. They steer our relationships, what we choose to share. They steal our joy, our voices, our energy. They don't just sit quietly. They pull us out to sea. But we don't have to let them anymore.

WHAT IS THIS STUDY ALL ABOUT?

Together in this study, we're going to identify the "core lie" that seems to be controlling the current of your life. This is about more than just insecurities you may be acting from. It's about *strongholds* this core lie made in your life and the very real enemy who operates within them. We're going to look at Matthew 4, where that enemy came at Jesus with lies—in an exchange known as the Temptation of Jesus that happened in the desert. We'll see how Jesus responded in truth and with authority, and we'll use His strategies to respond to our own lies. Then we'll do the work of replacing those lies with truth, positioning ourselves closer to the God of Truth who sets us free. When we do that? We'll see peace. We'll see confidence and flourishing. We'll see growth. We'll see what it's like to live as someone who is deeply loved. And we'll see that freedom spread to other people. God doesn't leave His children defenseless against these lies.

RESPOND

Coming into this study, what sense do you have of the lies you might be believing?

Have they been going on in the background unnoticed, or do any particular thoughts present themselves? If so, describe them.

What words are you using to describe yourself?

What decisions have you made about yourself?

What agreements are you making that might unintentionally box you in?

Whenever you catch yourself saying something disparaging about yourself, take a quick pause. What are you saying? Could you be believing a lie?

LIES VERSUS TRUTH

LIES

READ	RESPOND
John 8:43–44	How does Jesus describe our enemy?
Genesis 3:1–5	In Satan's first appearance in the Bible, what is he doing?
Revelation 12:9	How is the enemy described? What does he do in the world?

TRUTH

READ	RESPOND
John 1:12	What is your right as a follower of Jesus? What kind of safety does that give you?
Romans 12:2	How do we break from the pattern of lies in the world?
Hebrews 12:1	What do we have surrounding us? What does that empower us to do?

THE THREE CORE LIES

Those disparaging things we say about ourselves, those lies we believe, all boil down to three simple categories. And chances are, the lie that's directing your undertow will fall into one category more than the others. The lies are:

- I'm helpless.
- I'm unlovable.
- I'm worthless.

It sounds simplistic. But think about it.

The lie ***I'm helpless*** tells you that you have no control over what's happening to you. You are not up to dealing with life. So maybe you check out or avoid or numb out, all because you feel powerless in this crushing situation. You feel stuck—paralyzed, frozen in place. Maybe you silence yourself, shutting down your desires because you feel like it wouldn't make a difference in the face of the uncontrollable things happening to you. This lie keeps you small, believing you don't have what it takes.

The lie ***I'm unlovable*** tells you that you don't deserve to have good relationships. You worry you won't be accepted, so you double down and over-give in relationships, trying to offset that worry. But sometimes that goes wrong. And you end up accepting poor treatment from others as you search for connection. You brace for rejection, waiting for people to leave you, and hungry for proof that people care. You dread being hurt, so you try to please. But if anyone really saw you? *They'd leave*, the lie says.

The lie ***I'm worthless*** tells you that you'll never be good enough or get it together enough. No one notices you, your life doesn't matter, and you don't really contribute anything worthwhile. You have a hard time taking a compliment, because you don't think you're valuable. *You're a burden,* it tells you. *No one cares what you say. You don't matter, even if you try.*

I know it feels obviously wrong to think this way when it is laid out like this—but we still do it . . . all the time.

I think we all deal with each of these lies at some point in our lives, and different ones come to the fore at different times. But there is one lie that's taking the lead in your life right now. There's one that probably resonated with you as you read. That's where we're going to press.

PROJECT: IDENTIFY

Now let's make this personal. Pause with your group, take a break, and take this online quiz that my team has put together to help you pinpoint the lie that is yelling at you the loudest.

On your phone or a tablet, scan this code:

Or on a laptop, visit jennieallen.com/lies-quiz.

When you receive your results, write your core lie on a piece of paper, sticky note, or 3 × 5 card that your leader has for you, and record it here.

My core lie is ____.

RESPOND

What age were you when you first felt this?

Where or who did it come from?

How did it make you feel? What belief did that plant in you?

What evidence did you find to support it?

CONCLUSION

Over these six weeks together, you and I will be swapping out the lies for truth. You are giving Jesus the broken parts of you, and He is giving you back the whole, restored, redeemed version of you. That's your new identity. No more shame. No more labels. No more lies.

Now, this doesn't mean everything will be perfect from here on out. It doesn't mean life suddenly gets easy. But it does mean you're stepping toward the Light. You're identifying the ailment and reaching for the cure. You're choosing to walk toward truth. And when you keep heading in that direction, it gets easier, and you get freer.

This is the work.

It's the central work of my life, and it ought to be the central work of yours.

This is the process of living in freedom: recognizing the lies, giving them to Jesus, and stepping into the identity He's been waiting to give you all along. Next week we'll explore how switching between those identities—truth and lies—is just as solid as walking between two different kingdoms. And we'll learn how to keep choosing the Kingdom of Truth. But for now, you've done it. You've handed over that lie. And there's no going back.

As we keep doing this work every time the lies show up, we'll find that God's Truth is what makes us free.

"But when anything is exposed by the light, it becomes visible, for anything that becomes visible is light. Therefore, it says,
'Awake, O sleeper,
    and arise from the dead,
and Christ will shine on you'"
(Ephesians 5:13–14).

That's what this Light does. It names things truthfully. It cuts through shadow and silence. And when you see it again—and I mean *really* see it—you start to remember who you are and Who has you.

SEE ::

Watch video Session 1: **IDENTIFY**.

Use streaming instructions on inside cover or DVD.

Take notes if you like.

ASK ::

Use Session 1: **IDENTIFY** Conversation Cards for group discussion.

Complete the STUDY and PROJECTS for Session 2: **KINGDOMS** before your next group meeting.

SESSION 2

KINGDOMS

Work through pages 29–51 on your own before your next group meeting and video teaching.

Imagine living in a world that's not what you thought it was. One that makes you look around and think, *Where am I? Is this real?*

It reminds me of the movie *The Truman Show,* starring Jim Carrey. Have you seen it? It's old but such a good one. In it, Carrey plays a guy named Truman who is literally living in a world that isn't real. It's fiction. And he doesn't know it. Ever since he was a baby, he's been living on a meticulously built TV set, and his life has been broadcast as a TV show. And he is just walking around, living his everyday life, with no idea that this isn't the real world. His town is a huge soundstage. His family, friends, neighbors—all actors. But, as he gets older, he realizes something's up. *Wait,* he thinks. How come he sees the exact same people walking the exact same way every morning? How come his wife sounds like she's advertising a product on TV when it's just the two of them talking to each other? How come everywhere he goes, everyone knows him . . . like he's the star of his very own show?

It really starts to get to Truman. To the point that one day, he can't handle these suspicions anymore. He decides to try to leave his town. He'll have to escape by boat, which is a real problem because he's afraid of water. But he's desperate. And he's mad. He's reached his limit. And once he sees that his *entire existence* has been built on falsehood, he's determined to get to the truth, which in this case is the outside world.

My favorite scene is the last one, when the producer of the show works up a wild, raging storm on the "ocean" Truman is sailing. The producer tries to get Truman to turn back, to return home, to slip back into his comfortable, lie-based life and just play along with the whole thing. Truman nearly drowns, but still, he stays the course. He craves the truth that badly.

And then, *bam.* He hits a wall. A literal wall—the side of a dome. It's painted with blue skies and puffy white clouds. A fake water line on the fake horizon.

Fake matchy-matchy crystal-blue seas. It's just as he suspected. He presses his hands against the wall of the sound stage that has been his whole world and, for a second, he just breathes it all in. Then he looks up. To his left. To his right. And that's when he sees a staircase that leads up to a door. He climbs out of his boat. He sets one foot and then the other on the bottom step. He walks right up to that door and steps through it. And he ditches the lie-life for good.

He's gone from one world to another. From a land of lies to the real world. He's stepped into something truer.

And that's what I want us to do.

THE KINGDOMS ARE REAL

In order for us to stop believing our lies, we need to look around at the land built on them and exit into a different place. To go from one place—to another. Because breaking free from our lies is not a matter of trying harder. It's not a matter of applying a Bible verse "truth" and waiting for it to work. It's not a matter of thinking our way out of it. We can't just will ourselves to believe truth or convince ourselves to stop believing untruth. We have to exit the land built on lies. We have to go from one place to another. Walk through the door of a Dark world and live in the Kingdom of Light—the Kingdom of Truth.

The Truman Show is a movie, a story that does what fiction does and helps us think about what's true. But this idea of two kingdoms is not a metaphor. It is real.

Hang with me here, because this is about to get cosmic.

There is a Kingdom of Darkness. A real one. And there is a Kingdom of Light. As real as the other.

The Bible talks about them. And not in a parable. In reality.

THE DARK KINGDOM

Look with me at Ephesians 6:11–12, which describes the Dark Kingdom:

> "Put on the whole armor of God, that you may be able to stand against the schemes of the devil. For we do not wrestle against flesh and blood, but against the rulers, against the authorities, against the cosmic powers over this present darkness, against the spiritual forces of evil in the heavenly places."

You might have heard this passage before, but pause a minute and think about what it means in the real world.

As a kid, I must have missed the week in Sunday school when they talked about standing against the schemes of the devil, about the cosmic powers of the Darkness. I do remember my youth pastor saying, "It's not good to talk about the devil too much or to think about the devil too much." Have you heard that? Have you thought that?

Honestly, though—what help is *that* advice? Once I started reading the Bible for myself, I couldn't help but notice that it does talk about the devil—a lot. It talks about Dark cosmic forces coming against us. And it doesn't stop there. It says that our struggle is not against flesh and blood.

Rulers, powers, authority—all words that describe not just foul spirits but foul spirits that have authority. In John and 2 Corinthians, the devil is called the ruler of this world.

"The *god of this world* has blinded the minds of the unbelievers, to keep them from seeing the light of the gospel of the glory of Christ, who is the image of God" (2 Corinthians 4:4, emphasis added).

"'Now is the judgment of this world; now will the *ruler of this world* be cast out'" (John 12:31, emphasis added).

"The *ruler of this world* is judged" (John 16:11, emphasis added).

For sure, Satan has been given authority here on earth. And even though we know how the story ends—he will be defeated, and God will prevail—for now, we're in the middle of the fight. It's messy, it's hard, and we see the Darkness all around us. Every day of our lives, there's a war going on, and we can either deny its existence or acknowledge that it's real and that we are the prize.

That's the reason we need to wake up to the lies that have been controlling us.

Because this world is the Dark Kingdom, and friends, we're living in it. This world is not neutral ground. It's bent toward the Darkness.

CULTURAL CONTEXT

Maybe you're thinking. *Hang on. This all feels a little too Dungeons & Dragons for me. I did not sign up for this.* I get it. But can we at least agree that it feels like something Dark is going on beneath the surface of everyday life?

Under the brokenness we all have, under the mental health issues, the addictions and temptations, the tensions in our relationships and families, doesn't it feel like something more is happening beyond what we can see?

That "something" is not a hallucination. It's the tenor of this world.

And Satan's hope is that we won't see *any of it.* That we won't know it's there. That we'll continue living in this world and not know there's another one outside it. That we'll keep living by the laws of the land under his dominion.

STUDY ::

Read Ephesians 2:1–10 and Colossians 1:13–14.

Read Ephesians 5:6–16.

Notice the difference between those who walk in the Darkness and those who walk in the Light. Note the differences here.

How does recognizing the patterns of Darkness empower you to overcome them?

Read 2 Corinthians 4:6.

Notice how God gave us His Light as a way for us to know Him and His glory more intimately. Take a few notes.

How can God's new Kingdom of Light encourage you not only to see the lie patterns in your life but to walk away from them and toward His Light?

Throughout Scripture, God paints a picture of this kingdom, determined to make sure we know what it's like. Read these verses, and record what each one says about the differences between the Darkness and the Light.

READ	DARKNESS	LIGHT
Isaiah 9:2		
John 1:4–5		
Matthew 5:14–16		
Revelation 21:23–25		

In Scripture, the Kingdom of Light is described as the opposite of the Kingdom of Darkness. And that kingdom belongs to Jesus.

The Bible records Jesus talking about His kingdom:

"'My kingdom is not of this world'" (John 18:36).

"'The kingdom of God is not coming in ways that can be observed, nor will they say, "Look, here it is!" or "There!" for behold, the kingdom of God is in the midst of you'" (Luke 17:20–21).

"'Truly, truly, I say to you, unless one is born again he cannot see the kingdom of God'" (John 3:3).

Once we become His, the door is open to us. We walk up and out of the Dark Kingdom, into His Light.

Paul describes this transfer in Colossians 1:13: "He has delivered us from the domain of darkness and transferred us to the kingdom of his beloved Son."

In Ephesians 5:8, he puts it like this: "For at one time you were darkness, but now you are light in the Lord. Walk as children of light."

Wait, "Jesus *has* delivered us?" "At one time [we] *were* darkness?" Those thoughts are past tense. This transfer from Darkness has *already occurred* for those who are in Jesus. We have total access to the Light. But because we live in this Dark world by default, living into the Light is our daily task.

That's the essence of us being *in* this world, but not *of* it, as Jesus said when He pled to God for His disciples:

> "'I have given them your word, and the world has hated them *because they are not of the world, just as I am not of the world.* I do not ask that you take them out of the world, but that you keep them from the evil one. They are not of the world, just as I am not of the world. Sanctify them in the truth; your word is truth'" (John 17:14–17, emphasis added).

Jesus knew His disciples (that's all of us who believe in Him) would be existing in the Dark Kingdom, where lies are the currency. And to defend us, He asked that God sanctify us in the truth.

Notice this: Jesus didn't ask that we would *believe* the truth. He asked that we would be *sanctified* in the truth. Being sanctified is something that happens *to* you. You are being purified and sanctified by God through the work of the Holy Spirit, not by how hard you try to believe the truth, but by your faith in the truth.

I don't think fighting lies is as simple as people may make it seem. The lies we believe—that we're helpless, worthless, unlovable—sink much deeper. So, when someone says things like, "Fight lies with truth," "I've got help in God," "I have worth in God," "I'm loved by God," they may seem like good Sunday school answers. But they don't go deep enough.

I spoke to a room full of ministry leaders recently, and I aired the question: "Do you think the way you're going to stop believing that lie is by believing the truth?" And I just left it there. Hanging. "You think that's the answer?" Everyone was so uncomfortable. *What is she saying?* Finally, I asked, "How hard have you tried? How hard have you tried to believe the truth?" Our ability to believe wholly is just insufficient.

While we're living in the Dark Kingdom, where the laws of Darkness are active, simply believing the truth as hard as we can is not going to be enough. We've got to live under the power of a different kingdom, walking in a counter reality. We are spinning our wheels in the Dark, trying to sanctify ourselves in the truth. We need to go to a whole new place in our minds, hearts, spirits, and strength and breathe the air of the kingdom promised and to come—be purified by God's love, and be renewed by the Ruler of His kingdom.

The Kingdom of Freedom, the Kingdom of Boundless Grace, the Kingdom of Light—this is the eternal kingdom where we live free from the grip of lies.

Living in the Kingdom of Light, there is no worry of disappointing God. You're already living by His will and His ways. You can be at peace like Jesus showed us how to. You can be confident that He is transforming you into the best possible version of yourself. Yeah, you'll still screw up, but you'll come to see setbacks as chances to grow.

LAWS OF THE DARK KINGDOM

LAW	YOUR RESPONSE
Stay distracted from what is true about God and what is true about you.	You must chase after success, popularity, and power, convincing yourself that your worth is found in the approval of others and the accolades you collect. Satan wants you to remain in a constant state of striving, where your identity is built on fragile things that just can't uphold a life.
Stay isolated and in a state of despair.	In this place of Darkness, you feel stuck, forgotten, as if your pain is unique and unbearable. You forget that in truth, you are never alone. Others have walked through similar struggles, and God is always with you, ready to cross your path with theirs, ready to lift you out of despair.
Stay spiritually stuck and immature.	You must be content with surface-level faith, never digging deeper into God's Word or your relationship with Him. You're off-center, off-kilter, off your game. You're not operating in the strength and stability that comes with the truth God offers.

I hate these laws. And God hates them too. He hates the bondage, the striving, the way living under our lies keeps us stuck. If these are the laws of the land, we have to get out of here.

LAWS OF THE LIGHT KINGDOM

LAW	YOUR RESPONSE
Have Faith in God.	"And without faith it is impossible to please God, because anyone who comes to him must believe that he exists and that he rewards those who earnestly seek him" (Hebrews 11:6 NIV).
Depend on God.	"I lift up my eyes to the mountains—where does my help come from? My help comes from the LORD, the Maker of heaven and earth" (Psalm 121:1–2 NIV). "'For I am the LORD your God who takes hold of your right hand and says to you, "Do not fear; I will help you"'" (Isaiah 41:13 NIV).
Walk with God.	"You shall walk in all the way that the LORD your God has commanded you, that you may live, and that it may go well with you, and that you may live long in the land that you shall possess" (Deuteronomy 5:33). "Even though I walk through the valley of the shadow of death, I will fear no evil, for you are with me; your rod and your staff, they comfort me" (Psalm 23:4).

<table>
<tr><td>Rest in God.</td><td>“And he said, ‘My presence will go with you, and I will give you rest’” (Exodus 33:14).

“‘Be still, and know that I am God. I will be exalted among the nations, I will be exalted in the earth!’” (Psalm 46:10).</td></tr>
<tr><td>Trust God.</td><td>“Trust in the LORD with all your heart, and do not lean on your own understanding. In all your ways acknowledge him, and he will make straight your paths” (Proverbs 3:5–6).

“‘But blessed is the one who trusts in the LORD,
whose confidence is in him.
They will be like a tree planted by the water
that sends out its roots by the stream.
It does not fear when heat comes;
its leaves are always green.
It has no worries in a year of drought
and never fails to bear fruit’” (Jeremiah 17:7–8 NIV).</td></tr>
</table>

Love God.	"'Love the LORD your God with all your heart and with all your soul and with all your might'" (Deuteronomy 6:5). "'Love the Lord your God with all your heart and with all your soul and with all your strength and with all your mind, and love your neighbor as yourself'" (Luke 10:27 NIV). "This is love for God: to keep his commands. And his commands are not burdensome" (1 John 5:3 NIV). "'Whoever has my commands and keeps them is the one who loves me. The one who loves me will be loved by my Father, and I too will love them and show myself to them'" (John 14:21 NIV).

God is constantly beckoning us to that second kingdom. He's begging us never to leave it, because He knows it's where we're meant to be. All those times in Scripture when He says "fear not" or "take courage" or "come to me" or "rest" are divine invitations to exchange an old land for a new, Darkness for Light. To be set free. And in the process, we set others free.

RESPOND

Coming into this study, what have you heard or been told about Satan and his reality?

In what way are you used to dealing with the idea of his existence?

Considering your life today, what is the evidence around you of a broken reality? Where do you see Darkness operating? Where do you see the laws of the Dark Kingdom in action?

WHO ARE YOU, LORD? & WHAT DO YOU WANT FROM ME?

Read: Matthew 25:34. Considering what you read, answer the questions above.

DIGGING DEEPER

(OPTIONAL PROJECT FOR THOSE OF YOU WANTING TO GO DEEPER)

Read each passage below and list what you learn about the enemy from each section.

1. The Devil's Origin

- Isaiah 14:12–15
- Ezekiel 28:14–17
- Revelation 12:7–9

2. Who the Devil Is

- John 8:44
- 1 Peter 5:8
- 2 Corinthians 11:14
- 1 Thessalonians 2:18
- 1 John 3:8
- Matthew 4:1
- Revelation 12:10

3. What the Devil Does

- Genesis 3:1
- 2 Corinthians 4:4
- Ephesians 6:11–12
- Luke 22:31
- 2 Timothy 2:26
- Revelation 2:10

4. The Dark Kingdom

- Colossians 1:13
- Acts 26:18
- 1 John 5:19
- Ephesians 2:1–2
- Matthew 12:26

5. The Devil's Destiny

- Romans 16:20
- Revelation 20:10
- Hebrews 2:14

PROJECT 1

EXCHANGE

I want you to be able to find truth for the lies the enemy is telling you. So let's play a game: Read the descriptions of the Kingdom of Darkness. Then look up and read each description of the Kingdom of Light. For each Kingdom of Darkness phrase, draw an arrow to match the corresponding Kingdom of Light phrase.

KINGDOM OF DARKNESS	KINGDOM OF LIGHT
Built on lies and distortion	**Matthew 6:34** Delights in presence
Accuses, shames, and condemns	**John 1:17; 1 John 4:8** Built on truth and love
Runs on fear, control, and isolation	**Isaiah 54:10** Declares, "You are already loved"
Rewards performance	**John 16:13** Operates in clarity and light
Whispers, "You'll never be enough"	**Jeremiah 29:11** Awakens your purpose
Seeks to kill your purpose	**John 8:36** Came to set you free
Operates in hiddenness and confusion	**Colossians 1:13–14; Psalm 103:3–4** Forgives, restores, and redeems
Aims to enslave	**John 14:27; 2 Corinthians 3:17; Colossians 3:15** Runs on peace, freedom, and connection

PROJECT 2

WALK ON NEW GROUND

This project is simple but deeply impactful.

Take a walk. Imagine the Kingdom of God.

What is it like?

What are you like in it?

What is God like?

Now imagine your every day life and living in that kingdom here and now.

Ask God what it would be like to live like that.

Write your thoughts here after your walk.

PROJECT 3

DRAW IT OUT

Draw arrows into each body form identifying where you felt either the lie or the Light. Draw a shape, line, or symbol that represents how the lie and the Light felt in each corresponding part of your body you drew an arrow to.

FEELING THE LIE **FEELING THE LIGHT**

PROJECT 4

DECLARE

Declare what is true. Look up each Scripture passage below and complete the statement by putting the verses in first person as they define you. Then read the entire page aloud in proclamation of the truth over the lies and in declaration of the kingdom you live in.

I no longer live in the Dark Kingdom where:

I'm helpless.
I'm worthless.
I'm unlovable.

Instead, I live in the Kingdom of Light where:

Romans 8:11 tells me I ______________________________

______________________________.

2 Timothy 3:17 tells me I ______________________________

______________________________.

Romans 8:38–39 tells me that neither ______________________________

______________________________.

"The night is nearly over; the day is almost here. So let us put aside the deeds of darkness and put on the armor of light" (Romans 13:12 NIV).

CONCLUSION

"'And you will know the truth, and the truth will set you free'" (John 8:32).

When Jesus said the truth will set you free, He was saying you can be free from Darkness. Not the darkness of night, but the Darkness that controls this world. Satan will fight hard to keep you believing the lie. Your freedom matters, not just for your peace, but for your purpose—how your life affects the world.

Even if you're very intentionally trying to live in this Light Kingdom, to walk in God's calling, that doesn't mean you won't continue to face attacks from the enemy. Even Jesus faced those, as we will see next week in the desert temptation story. The hard reality is that sometimes we will face Satan at his worst. Sometimes we will struggle to see the Kingdom of Light when we're being pulled down by the Kingdom of Darkness.

The process of rejecting the lies doesn't just clear the fog; it uncovers the truth underneath—the truth that we are loved, we are worthy, and we can change. It can be hard. I know. It's painful. But each time we resist the pull of those lies, we exit the Dark Kingdom and claim our place in the Light Kingdom, and we create space for something deeper, something truer, to emerge.

Man. I just want you to catch that.

Something truer is about to emerge.

We become less influenced by what we're told we are and more connected to who we were made to be. And that clarity? It matters. Because it's in that clarity that we find peace, freedom, and the courage to move forward.

This fight is worth it in the end.

SEE ::

Watch video Session 2: **KINGDOMS**.

Use streaming instructions on inside cover or DVD.

Take notes if you like.

ASK ::

Use Session 2: **KINGDOMS** Conversation Cards for group discussion.

Complete the STUDY and PROJECTS for Session 3: **HELPLESS** before your next group meeting.

SESSION 3

HELPLESS

Work through pages 57–80 on your own before your next group meeting and video teaching.

I was sitting across from a friend of mine at a picnic table eating lunch, and I told her about the idea of all of us believing one of three core lies. She didn't even have to think about it before she told me what her lie was. She had suffered unthinkable abuse in childhood, and it took no time at all to figure it out. Her lie was *I am helpless.*

"I feel it all the time about everything," she said. "That's why it was so hard to break my addiction to porn and why I have never changed jobs, even though I have been so unhappy for so long. I'm helpless." She went on, having thought about this a lot already. "I know it comes from my childhood. I couldn't control what was being done to me. I know it's connected—it has to be. But I can't snap out of it, and this lie keeps crippling me. Season after season in my life, I'm just stuck."

She described how, on certain occasions, she'd experience victory and think that maybe she'd finally gotten over it. But the lie would eventually sneak back in, rendering her paralyzed all over again. A lot of us can relate to feeling helpless. And certainly, there are times when we cannot control our circumstances.

Whatever your core lie has been, we all know that feeling of resignation in the face of a bad situation—*I cannot get out of this. There is nothing I can do.* And for many of us, it started in childhood.

YOUR SIXTH-GRADE SELF

In this study, I'm asking you to take a trip back in time with me. To a point in your past when you first started believing the lies that still echo within you. For me, it was around sixth grade, when I was twelve years old. For others, it might be earlier. At some point, something happened that made you say, *Oh. This is reality. And if that's how it is, I'm going to have to adjust.*

This is true for all the lies we've been talking about. They get to us young, when we're defenseless. Our enemy fights dirty.

Many of us remember the circumstances in which the gong struck for us. *Oh. Okay then.*

Maybe it was the idea, *No one's coming for me. I'm on my own.* Or, *I am completely unable to meet these circumstances. I will never get it together.* Or, horrifically, *I have no control over these bad things being done to me. And so I'll freeze, paralyzed, because I'm literally helpless right now.*

I imagine us as little kids, thinking these things. And it makes me want to cry. Because it's so unfair. And it's the root of a lie that paralyzes us: *I'm helpless.*

Of the three core lies, I want to tackle the feeling of being helpless first, because it is often the lie that makes us feel like nothing can ever change. And if we're stuck forever, then what's the point of life? It's exactly what the enemy wants us to believe.

LEARNED HELPLESSNESS

If you need proof of the battle going on around us, of the Dark Kingdom in action, consider those moments in childhood. Everyone has one. When as precious children we looked up, noticed the laws of the Dark land around us, and decide, *Welp. These are the rules. I've got to play along.* It's at this time when our lies take root. And science tells us our brains are particularly receptive at this very time.

Child development experts tell us that around ages six to twelve, we are in the stage of inferiority. *Inferiority* means inward focus. And then age twelve to eighteen is the stage of role confusion.[1] So, you're trying to individuate. You're aware. You're no longer just thinking about yourself. You're thinking about what others are thinking about you, and you're trying to try different roles toward adulthood. You're naturally looking around and looking for how "things are." The perfect time for a lie to sneak in. For that lie to seem like a logical conclusion given the facts of the situation.

This lie *I'm helpless* gets to me because I think the devil wants us all to feel completely inadequate and unable to move. And how many days do I have where that feels like the case? Some days I wake up and that's not true anymore, but there are days when it just feels true. *I can't change anything*, or *this won't get better*, or *there's nothing I can do.*

---

1. "Learned Helplessness," Psychology Today, https://www.psychologytoday.com/gb/basics /learned-helplessness.

Psychologists describe this as "learned helplessness," or when "an individual continuously faces a negative, uncontrollable situation and stops trying to change their circumstances, even when they have the ability to do so."[2]

That's the very essence of the Dark Kingdom's rules, which come at us through no fault of our own, when we're too young to notice. Of course we feel helpless. In a way, we very well might be.

But we don't have to stay there. If we cross into the Light, we learn that the helplessness the enemy wants us to stay stuck in? It may have felt true in that moment. But it is not true forever. We have agency. We have power.

And in Jesus, we have authority. He shows us how.

In the passage you're about to read in the STUDY section, Jesus shares an example of how we can fight back, showing how the King of the universe, the Son of God, fought lies and refused to be drawn into the Darkness.

---

2. Raleigh Souther, "Identity Vs Role Confusion in Adolescence: Essential Insights for Parents and Educators," *Mental Health Center of San Diego*, August 7, 2025, https://mhcsandiego.com/blog/identity-vs-role-confusion-in-adolescence-essential-insights-for-parents-and-educators/.

STUDY ::

Read Matthew 4:1–11.

RESPOND

How was Jesus feeling during this episode? How would Satan have expected that to affect Jesus' attitude?

How are you typically feeling when you find yourself believing you have to fix things? Why do you think Satan would pick that time?

In verse 3, how would you imagine the Tempter's tone of voice toward Jesus?

How does Jesus respond to the Tempter? What's His tone of voice?

Now look ahead: What does He say to Satan in verse 10?

What happens in verse 11?

What does this ending tell us about what God is like?

What does this say about how we, too, can speak to the Tempter?

In that dry, barren desert, Satan begins by saying, "If you are the Son of God, tell these stones to become bread" (Matthew 4:3 NIV).

Well, okay then. To me, this sounds like baiting. He's trying to wind Jesus up. It's a cruel mix of temptation and doubt. *Oh, You think God loves You? Why are You hungry then? You'd better fend for Yourself.* The enemy appeals to Jesus' desires. I mean, get hungry after a long afternoon and start craving a pastry, but forty days? But Satan doesn't just offer Jesus bread; he pokes at

His identity too. It's so like him. And he does the same thing to us. You and I could be minding our own business, when all of sudden we spiral into an outright identity crisis.

If you are really God's child, fix the problem.

If you are really God's kid, He would give you what you need, right?

If you are really God's child, you would get your life together. You would get control, and God would make it all work out . . . so you must not be God's child.

The taunting, the shaming—it's merciless. These are Satan's schemes. This is how lies grow into strongholds and people give up. The enemy is evil. His plans are to kill you, to steal any hope from your life, and to destroy any faith you have. This is why it feels sometimes like we're helpless against his attacks.

But there's another level here.

Underneath the lie *I'm helpless,* if we dig down, comes another lie in response:

I can take control. I can turn stones into bread. I've got to, because no one is coming.

And that's what Satan is focusing on here.

Here's the twist: Jesus will not agree to live by Satan's rules. This is how He answered the enemy: "It is written: 'Man shall not live on bread alone, but on every word that comes from the mouth of God'" (Matthew 4:4 NIV).

That answer has authority. Not "I can take control," but "I'm living in a whole different land, one where God has control. He's nourishing me."

Jesus wasn't just quoting Scripture or clapping back; He'd been living out the Word of God. Out there for forty days, He had been eating nothing but God's presence for breakfast, lunch, and dinner. Yes, He was hungry alright. But because He had been walking with God, He was radiating that power and authority that comes with God's presence. He was radiating the truth of Scripture and God's provision. He could say for sure, "This is what God is like."

SPIRITUAL AUTHORITY

How do we begin to shift things to become more like Jesus? We start by seeing our lives as belonging to God. And by seeing our Father as belonging to us. Our circumstances can spiral out of control and we can still remain peaceful, because our hope is not in whatever scrap of control we can gain. It's in the Source.

I know you'll probably get mad when I say this, but I promise this is one of the truths that will set you free: You are never going to get complete control over your life. You won't. I won't either. But let me be clear. We are far from helpless. If we could shift our aim from chasing control to chasing deeper surrender to Jesus, then we could enter into the wild adventure of radically obeying God no matter what, acting with greater confidence, fighting Satan's lies with no hint of fear as we take up the spiritual authority we have been given by God.

Helpless? No. *Powerful.*

"'Behold, I have given you authority to tread on serpents and scorpions, and over all the power of the enemy, and nothing shall hurt you'" (Luke 10:19).

"'Truly, I say to you, whatever you bind on earth shall be bound in heaven, and whatever you loose on earth shall be loosed in heaven. Again I say to you, if two of you agree on earth about anything they ask, it will be done for them by my Father in heaven. For where two or three are gathered in my name, there am I among them'" (Matthew 18:18–20).

Don't miss that. Spiritual authority is a powerful tool we need to overcome our lies. It's the hammer we need for pulling out the nails that have bound us to a wall of shame. And those verses in Matthew assure us that we aren't the source of this power. We don't have to be superheroes here. Not alone, but with our community, we seek God's power. The freedom is contagious. The enemy hates that.

It's easy to forget we have access to God's power and authority. But when you and I walk fully in our spiritual authority, so much is true of us.

We aren't insecure.

We don't obsess about ourselves.

We see the warring kingdoms. Our vision becomes clear.

We have empathy and compassion for other people's bondage.

We're excited to help others fight Darkness in their lives, and we see it more clearly in our own lives. We see the lies crumble all around us, and the Light shines through.

No, we are far from helpless. In fact, we literally have a *Helper*.

Jesus said, when His ministry on earth was nearly done:

> "'I tell you the truth: it is to your advantage that I go away, for if I do not go away, the Helper will not come to you. But if I go, I will send him to you'" (John 16:7).

He sent us that Helper in the Holy Spirit. The Holy Spirit also operates with God's authority:

> "'When the Spirit of truth comes, he will guide you into all the truth, for he will not speak on his own authority, but whatever he hears he will speak, and he will declare to you the things that are to come'" (John 16:13).

And He brings truth to our minds in a world full of lies:

"'The Helper, the Holy Spirit, whom the Father will send in my name, he will teach you all things and bring to your remembrance all that I have said to you'" (John 14:26).

If you need the help of the Helper, just ask. Pray to God right now. He will send you Help.

"'How much more will the heavenly Father give the Holy Spirit to those who ask him!'" (Luke 11:13).

Spiritual authority doesn't come from striving more. It comes from surrendering deeper, in staying in lockstep with the One who made you. When our souls move in sync with Jesus, when we walk with the Spirit in the Kingdom of Light, the lies we struggle with lose their grip.

What experience or knowledge do you have of the Helper? How have you thought of Him previously? How does He bring authority?

Freedom is available, but it's a war every day. What would it look like to live in freedom from the lie, I am helpless*?*

WHO ARE YOU, LORD? & WHAT DO YOU WANT FROM ME?

Read: Isaiah 40:29. In light of what you read, answer the questions above.

DIGGING DEEPER

(OPTIONAL PROJECT FOR THOSE OF YOU WANTING TO GO DEEPER)

TWO KINDS OF CONTROL

When we say the word control, we usually mean the power to manage outcomes or keep things from falling apart. But the Bible uses different words for very different kinds of control.

WORLDLY CONTROL	SPIRITUAL CONTROL
Kyrieuō / Katakyrieuō "to rule over," "to dominate," or "to lord it over"	*Enkráteia* "self-control"
Describes control exercised over people, circumstances, and outcomes.	Means inner mastery—Spirit-led strength over our own thoughts, desires, reactions, and choices.
Jesus referenced this kind of control when He said: "The rulers of the Gentiles lord it over them" (Matthew 20:25).	"The fruit of the Spirit is . . . self-control" (Galatians 5:22–23).
This is the control driven by fear—the need to manage everything to feel safe: relationships, situations, timelines, outcomes. It's grasping for power when we don't trust God's sovereignty.	God doesn't call us to control our world—He calls us to surrender so we can learn to govern our hearts.
Worldly control tries to manage others and outcomes.	Spiritual self-control surrenders what we can't control and chooses obedience in what we can.
Control reaches outward.	Self-control reaches inward.

1. *Where in your life do you feel the strongest need for control right now?*

2. *What emotion is driving that need beneath the surface?*

PROJECT 1

RECOGNIZING THE ENEMY'S TACTICS

Think back to the enemy's tactic with Jesus in the desert. The enemy came at Him with a straight-out taunt. "*If* you are the son of God, tell these stones to become bread" (Matthew 4:3 NIV, emphasis added). He came to Jesus tempting Him to just fix the problem.

Guess You're powerless . . .

Guess You're helpless . . .

God's not helping . . .

Why don't You fix it?

In Revelation 12:10, the devil is described like this: "For the accuser of our brothers and sisters, who accuses them before our God day and night, has been hurled down" (NIV).

He is an accuser.

Fill in the chart on the next page.

In the left-hand column in the chart on the next page, list how you feel when you are at your most helpless.

In the right-hand column, write the taunts the enemy might be trying to pass off as your own voice.

HOW IS THE ENEMY MAKING YOU FEEL?	HOW IS THE ENEMY ACCUSING YOU?
ex. Exhausted	ex. You'll never be able to get everything done. You are not up to the task of living life.
ex. Abandoned	ex. It's all up to you now. You have to pull it all together, without any help.

Looking back on the childhood experiences that supported the lie you believe—whether it's *I'm helpless*, *I'm worthless*, or *I'm unlovable*—what experiences backed that up? How does the enemy make you feel? Fill in the chart below.

HOW IS THE ENEMY MAKING YOU FEEL?	REAL EXPERIENCES THAT SUPPORT THIS
ex. I feel helpless.	ex. Sickness, being very small, abuse, neglect, no one listens, etc.

A note on mental health and abuse: If your childhood experiences include abuse or trauma and remembering them right now has sent you on a spiral of pain, I am so very sorry. You bore the brunt of sin and the brokenness of people in your life. This process might feel impossible right now, because your mind and body have learned abuse and neglect, but God is the opposite.

I am so brokenhearted for you, and I grieve that I can't just bring wholeness or healing to you right at this moment. But I believe and pray that God can. I pray that you do not leave Him. He is a just God and He hates abuse and all the things that were done to you. I encourage you: Do not live in isolation with this. Share it with someone today, whether it's a counselor, a mental health professional, or a trusted friend for prayer. Hold on. And if all else fails, go back to the simplest answer, one that even a child can trust: *Jesus loves me, this I know.*

Once we realize that these are taunts, lies, and tactics, their power over us begins to fade.

PROJECT 2

SURRENDERING LIES TO JESUS

Take a moment for a centering prayer.

With both feet on the ground, place your hands on your lap, palms up. Take three deep breaths—breathe in and out.

Picture Jesus sitting across from you. Tell Him the lies you've believed/ are believing, the ones you listed above.

What has the enemy been "tempting" you to do or not do in response to these lies?

Look at Jesus. How is He viewing you? How is He looking at you? What emotion do you imagine Him feeling toward you?

Pray these words out loud:

I give You these weeks. Set me free. I lay down the fight before You and ask You to be the One to tell me how to see it, how to fight it, how to move through it, how to submit to You, to Your power and authority. Amen.

PROJECT 3

COMPARE

Expectation *[noun]:* the act or state of expecting: **ANTICIPATION**[3]

Compare the expectations you face as a human being in this culture, living in the Dark Kingdom, to the expectations you have as a Christ-follower, living in the Kingdom of Light.

EXPECTATIONS IN THE DARK KINGDOM	EXPECTATIONS IN THE LIGHT KINGDOM
ex. Succeed, excel, make money, get approval, etc.	ex. Be accepted, be given authority, etc.

"But to all who did receive him, who believed in his name, he gave the right to become children of God, who were born, not of blood nor of the will of the flesh nor of the will of man, but of God" (John 1:12–13).

"'Behold, I have given you authority to tread on serpents and scorpions, and over all the power of the enemy, and nothing shall hurt you'" (Luke 10:19).

3. *Merriam-Webster Dictionary*, "expectation," last modified November 13, 2025, https://www.merriam-webster.com/dictionary/expectation.

PROJECT 4

FINDING YOUR FIGHTER VERSE

When you're feeling helpless, you need backup. So, you're going to find your fighter verse. Read each of the following verses on spiritual authority. Select the one that speaks the loudest to you, and write it out in your own hand on the next page. Memorize it. Make it yours.

"'The Lord will cause your enemies who rise against you to be defeated before you. They shall come out against you one way and flee before you seven ways'" (Deuteronomy 28:7).

"Put on the full armor of God, so that when the day of evil comes, you may be able to stand your ground, and after you have done everything, to stand" (Ephesians 6:13 NIV).

"For the weapons of our warfare are not of the flesh but have divine power to destroy strongholds" (2 Corinthians 10:4).

"Do not be overcome by evil, but overcome evil with good" (Romans 12:21).

"For God gave us a spirit not of fear but of power and love and self-control" (2 Timothy 1:7).

I praise you because I am fearfully and wonderfully made; your works are wonderful, I know that full well" (Psalm 139:14 NIV).

"God is our refuge and strength, a very present help in trouble" (Psalm 46:1).

My fighter verse is:

CONCLUSION

Earlier in this guide, you took a trip back in time with me and observed your young self—the girl who was so susceptible to what the world was whispering to her. Picture her in your mind. Feel that gut punch as she starts to believe the lie *I'm helpless.* Now let's try something else. Flash forward. See yourself at eighty years old, holding that sweet kid self, and helping her. What would you say? What would you do?

Your future self, she's strong. She's quick to bring things to the Lord. She's quick to bring them to other people. She's walking in the authority granted to her by the Spirit of God, and she is a fierce prayer warrior. She's living in a full relationship with God. It's like she's getting her nourishment—her daily bread—from Him. When she feels helpless, she knows where to go. She knows about the enemy's taunts and temptations to turn stones into bread, to try to fix and control. And she knows exactly what to say to that: "I'm not living in your kingdom. I'm living on every word that comes from the mouth of God."

Imagine her pulling that little kid self in close, and with so much compassion, letting the little version of herself borrow her calm, letting peace pass from her aged body to that young person.

She can wrap her arms around that girl and say, "I've leaned into this. I've learned not to be afraid. Your hands aren't tied. You aren't paralyzed. You belong to a powerful, powerful God. You can stand up to that lie with truth. You are a citizen of a different kingdom. And you can rest in Him."

Believe it. Because it's true.

SEE ::

Watch video Session 3: **HELPLESS**.

Use streaming instructions on inside cover or DVD.

Take notes if you like.

ASK ::

Use Session 3: **HELPLESS** Conversation Cards for group discussion.

Complete the STUDY and PROJECTS for Session 4: **UNLOVABLE** before your next group meeting.

SESSION 4

UNLOVABLE

Work through pages 87–111 on your own before your next group meeting and video teaching.

If there's one thing we know about children, it's that they thrive on love. They deserve it and need it in the most basic developmental way. Of course, we all need love, no matter what age, but for children love is so visceral. And most people can't help but give it to them. We want to scoop them up and squeeze them and love on them. We see how Jesus loved on them in the Bible. We even sing it over them from the time they're little: "Jesus loves me, this I know."

Yet somewhere along the way, often at that tender childhood point we've been exploring, we get the message: *There's something about me that makes me hard to love. I'm the problem. I'm unlovable.*

"WHAT'S WRONG WITH ME?"

Take Lily. When she was seven, her parents got a divorce, and during one of her father's phone calls with his attorney, Lily overheard her dad say, "I can't stay here with Lily and her mom. I need to find a new place to live." It wasn't the truth, but Lily interpreted her father's comment to mean that she was somehow the problem. In her young heart, she'd become unlovable, a lie she deals with still today.

Or my friend Sarah. She told me that as she grew up, she always felt like one of the unlovable ones. When I asked what age that started, and if she remembered the moment, she said, "I was twelve." There's that age again. It was when her sister's health fell apart, and her whole family went to her aid. "But I was okay," Sarah said, "so I sat patiently in the waiting room while they went to her. And it hit me, *If everybody I love is over there in that room together, and they're okay, I'm okay here alone in this room by myself.* She said, "That's my image of life. I think, *If everybody's okay over there in that room, I'm okay right here.*"

Somehow that translated into the thought, *As long as God loves and takes care of those people, I don't even expect love. I don't deserve or expect care.* So, she's walked through life trying to be the one who is always "okay," but actually feeling completely unlovable and abandoned.

Maybe for you it was being picked on or bullied. *People just don't like me, and that's not going to change. I'm unlovable.*

Or maybe it was because you were different. *Something's wrong with me. I'm so defective. No one could ever love a weirdo like me.*

Or maybe you were abandoned or rejected by someone you should have been able to depend on. *They'll leave me. They don't love me. So, I must be unlovable.*

Tell me if reading those thoughts tears at your heart the way it does mine. Imagine those innately lovable, huggable, vulnerable children and the despair that comes with them drawing that conclusion.

And then those conclusions living on. For decades. Until we are where we are today. With a lie embedded in us that we can't shake. *I am unlovable.*

WHEN THE LIE GROWS UP

When I asked some of the women in my community about what feels true to them, their lies came out like this:

- *I'm "too much."*
- *I'm not valuable because I wasn't loved by my parents.*
- *I have to "be better" for God to love or accept me.*
- *I'm an inconvenience to everyone around me.*
- *My good friends really do not like me.*
- *There's no one who could truly love me.*
- *I need to earn love by not causing waves.*

Sound familiar? We've all felt unlovable at some point. And if this is your core lie, you've built your world around it. It flavors your relationships and your every interaction.

- *You don't feel worthy of closeness or the relationships you dream of.*
- *You don't feel secure in relationships, maybe giving too much to them, people-pleasing to keep things going, or accepting poor treatment as just "the way things are."*
- *You are on edge, because you think people are going to ditch you.*
- *You might avoid real intimacy and emotional vulnerability, because you don't want them to see how unlovable you are.*

- *You might find ways to soothe your anxiety by pushing people to prove their love for you. You test them, to see how much they care.*

Our natural need for love finds another outlet, and trickles through to the deeper lie: *I can be the person they would love. If only I were . . .*

So, we try to be useful. Be beautiful. Be "okay." Be better. Be someone that strives.

Satan can work with that.

LOOKING FOR PROOF

Our enemy excels in handing us "proof" that we are unlovable. It seems so obvious in the Dark Kingdom. *Oh, that's why people don't like me.* We see proof in our relationships with other humans. And in our relationship with God too.

Craving love from God, we look for proof. We test.

If God really loved me, why are things so hard?

If God really loved me, I wouldn't feel this way.

If God really loved me, He would have brought me what I need, what my heart desires so deeply in life.

But Satan whispers,

He's holding out on you. He must not love you. If He did, He would prove it. We'd all see it.

And it echoes in the lie, *I am unlovable.*

Satan has been at this a long time. And this is a trick he pulled on Jesus Himself. Back in the desert of the temptation, he made his classic move. And Jesus showed us how to fight back. He showed us what happens to that lie when it's dragged into the light of a different kingdom.

STUDY ::

Read Matthew 4:5–7.

Read Matthew 4:5–7 (NIV):

> Then the devil took him to the holy city and had him stand on the highest point of the temple. "If you are the Son of God," he said, "throw yourself down. For it is written:
>
> "'He will command his angels concerning you,
> and they will lift you up in their hands,
> so that you will not strike your foot against a stone.'"
>
> Jesus answered him, "It is also written: 'Do not put the LORD your God to the test.'"

Satan was trying to convince Jesus to test the Father.

If God really loved You, He'd catch You if You jumped.

If God really loved You, He'd do it so everyone could see, with angels and everything.

See? The Bible even says it.

Do it now. Force His hand. Then we'll see how much You are loved.

Satan tried to use Scripture and twist it, but Jesus responded by quoting Scripture. And not only that, He responded with a Kingdom of Light view on who God *really* is.

Jesus quoted a command given to God's people in Deuteronomy 6. It wasn't an arbitrary rule. It was part of "The Greatest Commandment" God delivered to Israel, given as God was bringing His people out of slavery. It was one of the rules for the people to follow as they entered into and inhabited the promised land, to keep them safe. To keep them within the protection and will of God's best for them.

Jesus knew the consequences of living outside of God's will and protection and goodness. And He knew it started with testing Him. The Israelites had been "testing" God in the desert, and it was causing needless delay on their way to what God had for them. God just wanted to be good to them, and for them to trust Him.

Jesus was referencing **Deuteronomy 6:10–12**:

> "And when the Lord your God brings you into the land that he swore to your fathers, to Abraham, to Isaac, and to Jacob, to give you—with great and good cities that you did not build, and houses full of all good things that you did not fill, and cisterns that you did not dig, and vineyards and olive trees that you did not plant—and when you eat and are full, then take care lest you forget the Lord, who brought you out of the land of Egypt, out of the house of slavery."

That's remembering who God is. Who loves us, who is setting in motion His best for us, and is looking out for us. He's not holding out on us. He is for and with us.

How do we spot and fight a lie?

By remembering what is true of God.

Those things are true even when we don't feel them. Even when we're in pain. In this case, the truth that He is a loving father, and we don't have to earn that love.

RESPOND

What was Satan offering Jesus?

What "evidence" was Satan trying to use to convince Jesus?

What about Jesus' surroundings and situations would Satan have alluded to in order to suggest that God was holding out on Jesus?

If Jesus did what Satan suggested, what would this display "prove"?

How did Jesus respond?

What does His response say about who He knew God to be?

What does His response say about how God treats His children?

Why would confidence in that counteract Satan's strategic "evidence"?

"See what kind of love the Father has given to us, that we should be called children of God; and so we are" (1 John 3:1).

"By grace you have been saved through faith. And this is not your own doing; it is the gift of God, not a result of works" (Ephesians 2:8–9).

God is leading us somewhere. He's leading us out of slavery and into the promised land. Not testing means not getting stuck on what that *should* look like—*If God loved me, He would be doing X*—but simply accepting His love.

Jesus is essentially saying to Satan, "Why would I throw Myself off this tower to get God to prove He loves Me? I know He does. In My Kingdom of Light, that love is what we live on."

Plus, Jesus has some perspective. He doesn't throw Himself off the temple. But then, ultimately, He rises from the dead. He ascends to heaven, where He's at the right hand of God. One day, He will make all things right. God *will* lift Him up. The prophecy Satan cited about the angels will come true. It's just going to come true *later*. Jesus knows that God is taking Him somewhere. He's on His way somewhere. God's got a greater plan, so Jesus is not going to waste time in the desert by testing Him. He knows God, and He is confident that His Father loves Him. What a way to live!

But why is that confidence sometimes so hard for us to find?

GOD LIKES YOU

We know in our heads that God loves us. The problem, though, is that a lot of the time we can't believe—we just *can't*—that it's that simple. Unearned. Freely given. And not under duress. Not even because He has to.

Those of us with *I'm unlovable* as our core lie have trouble believing people really like us. We might get the feeling that someone is just being nice. Like at church—they *have* to be nice to you, right? Those are basic church manners. They couldn't possibly just enjoy you, could they? And the same with God. God *has* to love you, right? It's His job. He loves you because He's a good guy, but you're basically a charity case.

But here's the thing that shakes that lie:

God doesn't just love you; He also likes you. God likes you, your personality, your countenance, your quirks, your gifts and talents, your setbacks and insecurities, your foibles and failures and fears. **He finds you delightful**. And not just some future version of you, where you've got it together. Right now. He really, really likes you.

He didn't send His Son because you're inherently unlovable or gross or defective. He sent Him because He loves you. And likes you. Yes, you.

Need proof?

David said:

> "He brought me out into a broad place;
> he rescued me, because he delighted in me" (Psalm 18:19).

The prophet Zephaniah said:

> "The LORD your God is in your midst,
> a mighty one who will save;
> he will rejoice over you with gladness;
> he will quiet you by his love;
> he will exult over you with loud singing" (Zephaniah 3:17).

That's not a God who is phoning it in. He is not tolerating you. He is deeply, clearly, enjoying you.

When I really like someone, I hold their face in my hands and I tell them, "I like you." And honestly? That feels bigger than love. Because love is a have-to. We're *commanded* to love, after all. But *like* is something natural and organic that grows between people. And sometimes, that's all we need to remind us who God is to us. To you. He likes you.

When you spend time with Him, I pray you will feel this deep in your bones. That you would experience Him delighting in you. Because absolutely nothing compares to that. The longings and unmet dreams in our hearts, the things we think we need to feel loved, we can accept that our God is leading us somewhere better. When we feel abandonment, rejection, brokenness, alienation that feeds the *I'm unlovable* lie we know those aren't from Him. Because we know Him.

So, let's face the lie, offering to God the places that hurt. Because we know Him. And we know He is good.

What's your reaction to the idea that God likes you? Do you find it easy or hard to believe? Why?

What would feel different between being liked and loved by God for you? Based on how He made you, what does He like about you?

WHO ARE YOU, LORD? & WHAT DO YOU WANT FROM ME?

Read: Zephaniah 3:17. In light of what you read, answer the questions above.

DIGGING DEEPER

(OPTIONAL PROJECT FOR THOSE OF YOU WANTING TO GO DEEPER)

Do a deeper word study on the word *delight* in Scripture. What kinds of things does God delight in?

You can start with:

- Psalm 149:4

- Psalm 147:11

- Micah 7:18

- Proverbs 12:22

PROJECT 1

WRESTLING WITH UNMET DESIRES

We often want to test God because we have so many unmet desires and unexpected disappointments. Let's start by being honest. Read these prompts and then fill out the chart below recording the times of disappointment and unmet desires in your life that stand out to you the most.

What have you longed for that God hasn't done yet?

Have you ever felt like God is holding out on you? When was that?

DISAPPOINTMENTS	UNMET DESIRES

Complete this sentence in the way that connects most with those unmet desires: If He really loved me . . .

What are you afraid of when you look at this list?

PROJECT 2

SEEING GOD'S LOVE IN YOUR LIFE

Think back to those times you just identified. Consider what else may have been going on at the time.

- *During those times of disappointment, where did you see God show up? How was He helping you? Sparing you? Leading you?*

- *List three instances of His faithfulness.*

- *How has God shown you He loves you?*

All the times He did show up. All the times He kept me. He showed His love by those same actions.

PROJECT 3

IDENTIFYING EARLY LIES

What age were you when you first felt unlovable?

Describe the situation. What voice or circumstance made you feel that?

How did you react to that situation? How did it make you feel?

What agreements did you make with the ideas that came out of that situation?

How has that agreement affected your life?

Read Ephesians 2:1–10, *keeping your answers to those questions in mind.*

What are the characteristics of the Dark Kingdom described in this passage?

What changed when Christ rescued you from that Darkness?

Why did Christ save you?

According to verse 10, what does He have in store for you?

What can you know about *who God is* that will help you break agreement with the lie that you are unlovable?

PROJECT 4

RECLAIMING YOUR IDENTITY

Prayer for Healing

Take some quiet time by yourself to pray a powerful prayer for healing. Let this prayer guide you to offer God your wounds and help you open up to live free of lies. Consider what you've revealed about the painful moments in your past, and sit with your Father in a quiet place free of distractions. Pray for:

▶ ***Presence***

Jesus, would You still my heart and help me to come fully present to You?

I invite You into my broken places, especially my event from Project 3, and the times I've felt unlovable. Bring Your Light to my heart. You have authority there.

(2 Corinthians 4:6)

▶ ***Authority***

I exercise the authority of Christ over all other voices that seek to speak to me. In the name of Jesus Christ, I command you, Satan, and all other influences to be silent and not interfere. I belong to the Kingdom of Light.

(Speak your fighter verse, page 79)

▶ ***Searching***

Father, Son, Holy Spirit, would You come in a special way and minister deeply in my heart? My heart is not a puzzle to You, God. Would You search it and bring up one painful wound that needs Your healing touch?

(Psalm 139:23–24)

▶ ***Communication***

Lord Jesus, would You please communicate with me during this time? Open my eyes to how You are speaking to me.

(Jeremiah 33:3)

After praying this prayer, wait in silence and avoid the tendency to analyze. Instead, trust God from the bottom of your heart. Don't try to figure out everything on your own.

▶ ***Freedom***

I now break agreement with the lies I've believed. I reject them. I choose to leave the Darkness and live in the Light.

(James 4:7)

▶ ***Healing***

Lord, please heal this place in my heart. Only You can work miracles. Show me what it means to live loved by You, secure in Your affection, and whole in Your healing.

(Jeremiah 17:14)

In Jesus' name, amen.

CONCLUSION

When my kids were little, I used to watch *Mister Rogers' Neighborhood* with them. It wasn't just good for their little hearts—it was good for mine too! I love how Fred Rogers gave us that slow, gentle show on PBS that moved at the speed of trust, full of kindness and space to just be. It was a beautiful place for kids and their vulnerable, sweet, curious hearts.

There's one episode that's stuck with me over the years, one I still think about often. In it, Daniel Tiger—this quiet, tender little tiger puppet—has a conversation with Lady Aberlin, one of the human characters on the show.

Daniel is struggling with some big feelings, and he begins asking the question that so many of us, in our own way, are still asking quietly in our hearts: *"Am I a mistake?"* He lists all the things that make him feel different and out of place—how he doesn't have stripes like other tigers, how he lives inside a clock, how he feels awkward and unsure of where he fits.

In response, Lady Aberlin looks at him with compassion and sings these words over him:

"Despite all your differences, you're not a mistake.
I like who you're becoming.
And when you're asleep or when you're awake . . .
I like you."[4]

The beauty of this episode is in its simplicity. But it's also profound.

---

4. *Mister Rogers' Neighborhood*, season 15, episode 78, "Mistakes: Daniel and Lady Aberlin," written by Fred Rogers, directed by Paul Lally, aired May 6, 1987, on PBS.

Something in me still melts every time I hear those words, because whether it's coming from a puppet show or the pages of Scripture or the whisper of the Holy Spirit in a quiet moment—we all need to be reminded again and again that we are not a mistake. And that God not only loves us in some abstract, theological way, He actually *likes us*.

He likes you when you're asleep, when you're not performing, when you're not proving anything to anyone. He likes you even when you're still healing. He likes you in the middle of your mess.

And I want you to hear this clearly: That's not just something nice to make you feel better. That truth—*that God delights in you*—is the beginning of real, lasting freedom.

You don't need to test, to strive, to be anything other than what you are right now to get that. You are loved. Liked. Enjoyed. Treasured. Feel that in your bones, and let it bring you to life. And drag the lie that you are unlovable into the light.

SEE ::

Watch video Session 4: **UNLOVABLE**.

Use streaming instructions on inside cover or DVD.

Take notes if you like.

ASK ::

Use Session 4: **UNLOVABLE** Conversation Cards for group discussion.

Complete the STUDY and PROJECTS for Session 5: **WORTHLESS** before your next group meeting.

SESSION 5

WORTHLESS

Work through pages 117–142 on your own before your next group meeting and video teaching.

This week is personal for me. The lies we've been talking about? We're about to dig into the one that shouts loudest at me—the lie that *I am worthless*. And, of course, it started early.

I've mentioned before that this all started when I was about twelve years old. I tell this story a lot, and I cringe every time I do. Because it has to do with my dad, whom I love deeply. I would never blame him, but it's one of these crystalized moments that hits us when we're kids, and Satan latches on.

Basically, I was twelve, perched on my dad's lap in his recliner. We were just sitting there, the way we always did. Him stretched out long and tall, me awkwardly draped across his chest, my legs dangling over the wide arm of the chair. Both of us staring up at the popcorn ceiling like it was a starry night. We'd talk like that. Ideas. Hopes. Dreams.

But something changed as I got older. It became harder to find things we had in common—and that's when the questions started. He meant no harm. I know that now. But back then, what I felt—what I knew—was that there were categories in life. And those categories came with expectations. Whether he was asking me about boys or grades or sports, I never quite seemed to clear the bar.

I got the idea that there were marks I had to reach. That I wasn't measuring up. If I didn't achieve, I'd be a disappointment. So I had to excel. Be great. Be impressive and shiny and get all the middle-school accolades. Otherwise, I wouldn't be worth much at all. I'd be worthless. *Well, this is how it goes. Hit the marks and succeed, or you're not worth anyone's time.* My dad and I have had long, healing conversations since then—God has brought so much grace between us—but this is the piece I want you to see. That high bar I felt growing up? It didn't come from nowhere. It came from somewhere real—my dad's own story. His own ache.

MAKING THE GRADE

I'd been looking to my dad to bring me worth, which of course he could not do. I'd weighed his words far heavier than what he'd intended and then blamed him when they were too much for me to carry at that tender age.

But Satan is a gross opportunist who forever looks for weakness to exploit. And, boy, did he find it in me.

"You will always be a disappointment," he'd whisper.

This lie echoed through me. It continued in the background for many years. Like I said, eventually my dad and I had healing conversations about it, and we have both tasted freedom from the lie. But when I was a kid, the lie formed the way my brain works. Let me tell you how.

Every day, in every small part, I judge my life. Subconsciously, without meaning to, I evaluate how I did. *Was it good enough?* I judge how I comforted you in one of the talks I've given. *What score would you give me?* Or how I performed in a meeting. *How was I on that phone call? Did I listen enough?* I'm judging and scoring my life—*all the time.*

I had a conversation with my counselor, Kurt Thompson, about this, and he made an observation that rang so true. He said, "You have a scorecard in your head, Jennie. You're grading yourself all the time." Like some nightmarish outgrowth of my school days.

And it's true. Deep in my heart, I'm thinking, *There's a grade for everything, and I'm going to have to make it.* These days, I'm okay with some B's and I'm okay with an A minus in life, but believe me, that's a recent development. There was a time in my life where I needed to make all A's in everything I turned my hand to. I'm not that girl anymore, but in the background, I'm still judging myself against the marks I need to hit.

This bleeds into my relationship with God too. I have felt like I have to report to Him, and He's going to grade me. I have to be a success, or He's going to fail me. I'll be worthless. I secretly know that all my striving, all my wheel-spinning, is never going to be enough. In the end, it just won't. But that doesn't stop me from trying.

HOW THE LIE GROWS

Maybe you're like me. This lie shows up in sneaky ways for us that we may not have clocked, or realized, before.

- *We doubt whether we're noticed or whether we matter in the end.*
- *We struggle with praise and compliments.* If they knew what a mess I was, they'd be singing a different tune.
- *We think we're insignificant, and what we do isn't making a difference.*
- *When people try to tell us we're inherently valuable, it just never sinks in. It bounces right off.*
- *We feel like we'll never get it together, but asking for help is hard, because we're afraid we are a burden.*

When I asked the women in my community, they said *worthless* speaks to them like this:

- *I am unworthy. Unworthy of other people's belief in me.*
- *My opinion is not really worth anything, so I might as well be quiet.*
- *I'm not worthy of being loved.*
- *I can't share my disappointments because others have it worse than me.*
- *My worth is based on how much I do for others.*
- *If I can't be excellent, I might as well not even try.*

Now, if we were playing the opposites-game, the obvious way to combat this lie would be, "Of course you're worthy! You have such inherent worth."

To which I would smile tightly, say thank you, and tell you how sweet you are to say that. Then walk off and keep doing the same old things in my head with my scorecard.

Because of course that's true. We all have inherent worth. But for some reason, that doesn't echo in my soul. At least not as loud as the lie does.

In that situation when we're falling under harsh judgment and feeling worthless and scrambling to do something significant, we need to know that God is compassionate. We need to know that He gets it. We need to know that Jesus was tested too. That He has faced this lie, and He knew what to do about it. And He shows us how too.

STUDY ::

Read Matthew 4:8–11.

This third encounter is the last temptation in the desert. It's Satan's big guns—the final attempt to take out the Son of God before Jesus' ministry begins.

The enemy had already tried to get Jesus to take things into His own hands: *If You are really God's child, You would get Your life together—You'd turn these stones to bread.* He'd tried to provoke Him to question God's love: *If God really loved You, life wouldn't be so hard—You'd jump and He would catch You.* After Jesus shut down both of these, Satan came after Jesus by offering Him significance.

"The devil took him to a very high mountain and showed him all the kingdoms of the world and their splendor. 'All this I will give you,' he said, 'if you bow down and worship me'" (Matthew 4:8–9 NIV).

He offered Him a kingdom now . . . here. Jesus wouldn't have to wait, and He wouldn't have to die on a cross. He could see that splendor now.

You all know which kingdom this is. The one we've been talking about. The Dark Kingdom that is the default mode of this world, even with all its splendor. And it was his to give. This is his territory.

Remember the enemy's rules in this world? We have to be significant. We have to measure up. Because, in his world, what we achieve and how we are viewed matters most.

Satan was offering Jesus the chance to be impressive. Kingly. A ruler. Not humble and hungry and hot in the desert.

All he wanted in return was Jesus' loyalty and devotion: *All this I will give you. If you remain in my world and play by my rules.*

But Jesus said to him,

> "'Away from me, Satan! For it is written: "Worship the Lord your God, and serve him only"'" (Matthew 4:10 NIV).

Jesus confronted the offer of worldly significance by declaring that He lived in a whole different kingdom. In essence, Jesus said, "We are made for God. We only find significance in knowing and worshiping him." And it worked!

Scripture then says,

> "The devil left him, and angels came and attended him" (Matthew 4:11 NIV).

God was going to care for Him anyway. Jesus just showed us how to stand up to the lie.

That's where I want to be. I want to be worshiping God instead of my good performance. I want to be in His kingdom. The lie *I'm worthless* has underneath it a deeper lie—*I can have worth by being significant.* In the Dark Kingdom, yeah. That's true. We can get a leg up if we display significance and success. We do get treated differently if we are killing it on the world's stage. That's a basic law of this kingdom, like gravity.

But Jesus is saying, "I don't live there. In My kingdom, we are too busy worshiping our amazing God and serving Him to worry about any of that." That scramble to achieve, that desperation—it's been replaced by confidence and trust in the One worthy of all our worship.

RESPOND

Why would this third temptation be the one to end on? From Satan's point of view, why is this the high point?

After forty days in the desert, before Jesus was about to begin His ministry on earth, why would this promise have been an attractive option?

When Satan makes his offer to Jesus, how does it sound to you? What is the enemy desperate for?

What did Jesus' answer say about who God is?

What did Jesus' answer say about who Satan is in comparison?

Describe what Satan did in response.

How does what happened next show how God cared for Jesus?

How does that also show God is worthy of worship?

We get to choose. Are we going to live in the land of striving and achievement, going for perfection and splendor? Or are we going to live in the land of love?

This choice reminds me of the story about Jesus later in His ministry, when He showed everyone again that He was operating under a completely different framework.

Read Mark 3:1–6.

I love the story of Jesus healing on the Sabbath, because He *knew* He was going to tick everybody off. They were playing by oppressive, man-made rules in a Dark Kingdom. But He asked them, *What do you really care about? What do you think is going to happen? Do you think I should heal on the Sabbath?* I think it was a kingdom conversation. *Which kingdom are you operating in?*

He knew what they were going to say; they were testing Him. He knew their motivation. But He was essentially asking them, *Are you going to live under this law or that law? The Dark Kingdom's law, or Mine? Are we going to hit marks here, or are we going to see God's healing power?*

Jesus is showing us, in the moment when there's a scorecard, when people are expecting things of us, to just be faithful. You don't need to be checking off boxes in your own mind or in anyone else's. He's just looking for you to come over to His kingdom and see His healing power and watch Him act.

NOT ENOUGH

Do you know what has worked for me? With my running scorecard, trying to make the top grade in life?

What's worked is the truth, where I rest, where I find comfort with my running narrative of getting an F.

To say, "I messed up and God loves me still. If anything, we're closer." I can bomb, and it's okay. I can fail, and it's not the end of the world. The freedom is that I don't have to perform, or I don't have to hit the mark, and that the gospel's true.

> "All have sinned and fall short of the glory of God, and all are justified freely by his grace through the redemption that came by Christ Jesus" (Romans 3:23–24 NIV).

Imagine the relief of not having to measure up and achieve and be as "splendid" as we can, all on our own. Those things are rules of the Dark Kingdom. But in the Light Kingdom, we get to lay down our burden, our scorecard, our frustration at never getting it right, and say, "God, I'm so glad You measure up for me."

We don't have to be "enough." He's enough.

That can be a hard, grit-your-teeth moment—to admit "I'm not enough." It sounds like low self-esteem. It hurts the ego. Or that you're phoning it in or taking the easy way out. Maybe everything in you is resisting it. But I ask you to consider: Could it be an invitation to let go? To be helped? To be held? The raw, real truth is, sometimes we are just not up to the task we are set, all on our own.

We're all in need of help, a Savior, a God who redeems and equips us for every good work.

"May the God of peace . . . equip you with everything good that you may do his will . . . through Jesus Christ, to whom be glory forever and ever" (Hebrews 13:20–21).

Through Jesus Christ. He equips. His will, His work, His strength. We do it through Him.

That's the heart of the gospel: Jesus died for our sins, because we weren't enough. And that's okay. He's taken care of it.

In the Prince of this world's kingdom, we feel driven to excellence to feel worthy, to be enough, to hit the mark. In the Kingdom of Light, though, we're not coasting. In fact, we're serving God with all our hearts:

"Whatever you do, work at it with all your heart, as working for the Lord, not for human masters, since you know that you will receive an inheritance from the Lord as a reward. It is the Lord Christ you are serving" (Colossians 3:23–24 NIV).

There's nothing wrong with giving it your absolute best and having high standards and a commitment to performing well. God loves us when we knock it out of the park. And at the same time, He loves us when we don't. This is the difference between the Dark Kingdom and the Light. We are motivated by who God is and what He's about.

Who would you be without your drive to achieve significance? In the Dark Kingdom?

How about in the Light?

WHO ARE YOU, LORD? & WHAT DO YOU WANT FROM ME?

Read: Psalm 145:3. In light of what you read, answer the questions above.

DIGGING DEEPER

(OPTIONAL PROJECT FOR THOSE OF YOU WANTING TO GO DEEPER)

Dig deeper into Hebrews 13:20–21.

- What are the descriptors of God in verse 20?

- What do those descriptions tell us about what God is like?

- How does that make Him uniquely qualified to equip us?

PROJECT 1

MEASURING YOUR WORTH

Think about your own personal scorecard. What has to happen for you to feel like you "hit the mark" in life?

Write down all the things you think you need to be in the circle on the right.

▶ *What are the expectations you've placed on yourself? Be honest.*

The bullseye always seems to be moving, and sometimes that's based on how people around me are doing. I look and I compare, and I add more to my list.

▶ *How has the mark been moving for you?*

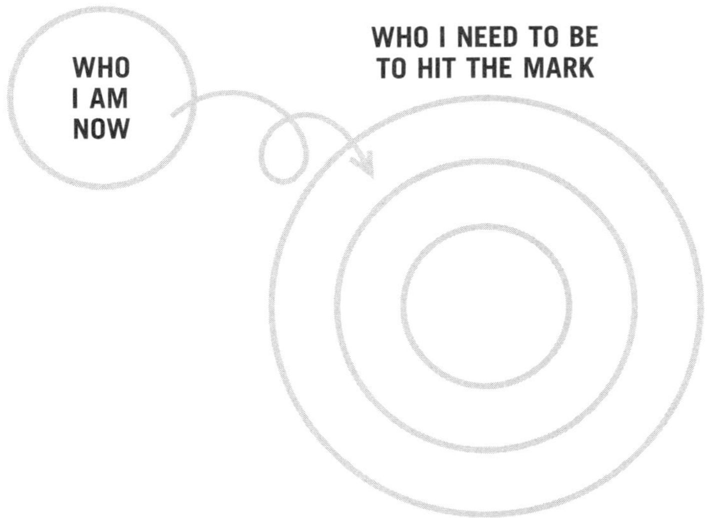

PROJECT 2

FACING FEAR

We're not just talking about made-up expectations in your head here. You have real expectations and responsibilities that are pressing—the ones weighing on your back, that are part of living your everyday life. You can't get rid of those.

I can hear you say, "There are things I have to do, I'm striving to achieve, and I can't do it all."

I bet that's true. As you write your list, pray: *Is there anything God is asking me to lay down?*

WHAT ARE THE REAL EXPECTATIONS YOU HAVE?	WHERE ARE YOU STRIVING?	WHAT CAN YOU LAY DOWN?

What are you afraid of if the worst happens and it all crashes down?

Read Psalm 18:1–19.

What was happening to the psalmist?

How did God react?

What did He make happen?

How did He treat the psalmist?

Why did He do this?

PROJECT 3

REMEMBER

What age were you when you first felt worthlessness?

Describe the situation. What voice or circumstance made you feel that way?

How did you react to that situation? How did it make you feel?

What agreements did you make with the ideas that came out of that situation?

How has that turned into action in your relationships and your life?

"But he said to me, 'My grace is sufficient for you, for my power is made perfect in weakness.' Therefore I will boast all the more gladly of my weaknesses, so that the power of Christ may rest upon me. For the sake of Christ, then, I am content with weaknesses, insults, hardships, persecutions, and calamities. For when I am weak, then I am strong" (2 Corinthians 12:9–10).

PROJECT 4

BENEVOLENT DETACHMENT

Practice becoming more detached from the outcomes of the things you're striving for. It's a safe way to stretch yourself, with love as the foundation, to let go.

THEN WHAT?

Play a few rounds of the "Then what?" game. You could write it out, or even invite a friend or loved one to sit with you and talk you through it.

The game goes like this:

- *Take one of your fears from Project 2, or something that plagues your mind that you think might happen if you stop striving.*
- *Ask, "Then what?" What would happen if that actually occurred?*
- *Continue to play out this scenario, asking, "Then what?" as many times as you can.*
- *What's the ultimate end?*
- *What does it mean in this scenario to have God's approval, despite your success or failure?*

EXPERIENCE

In the Kingdom of Light, you are offered security in God's approval regardless of success or failure.

Practice speaking truth over your lie of worthlessness. Look up and read each verse listed below. Then rewrite the verse starting with, *Even if I fail . . .* Finish it with each verse's content written in first person.

Example: **1 Peter 2:9**

Even if I fail, **I am a** *chosen race, a royal priesthood, a holy nation, a people for his own possession, that* **I might** *proclaim the excellencies of him who called* **me** *out of darkness into his marvelous light.*

Read and rewrite Isaiah 43:4.

Even if I fail, ____

____

____.

Read and rewrite Luke 12:6–7.

Even if I fail, ____

____

____.

Read and rewrite Ephesians 2:4–9.

Even if I fail, ____

____

____.

Read and rewrite Psalm 73:26.

Even if I fail, ____

____

____.

CONCLUSION

There's nothing like the benefit of hindsight, is there?

We all have this moment when the lie enters and we believe it. Mine was at twelve years old in a semi-insignificant conversation with my dad. I heard a lie that went on to shape the lie I still struggle with today.

When did you first believe the lie?

How old were you?

I swore up and down I would make sure my kids never got this same idea from me. But guess what? Somehow, through this Dark Kingdom or through some kind of parenting pendulum swing, my daughters absorbed this lie as their own. The idea that they have to be awesome, or they're worthless. Hide their mess, or they're worthless. The devil is coming at them with this garbage. It has got to stop.

How do we break this cycle? For me, for you, for the light and life of those we love?

My counselor is challenging me on this right now, saying that when we get to that moment where we're looking back on our lives and can see our journey, that can be a moment of healing. We can't progress or heal until parts of ourselves have dealt with the reality of what we've been through.

So, that's what we're doing here. We're going back and looking at things in God's Light instead of the Dark. God invites us to see. He looks at our hurt and striving hearts and says, "Let's go there. Let's look. Because I bet believing that made it hard for you sometimes to pray or to be close to Me. And that's what I want for us."

We can be weak in front of Him. We can bring Him our what-ifs and striving hearts and trust Him to heal us. He's not interested in our checking boxes. In our being significant. We could be a beggar or the monarch of all the kingdoms in all the world in all their splendor—still, all He'd care about would be a relationship with us. He's not going by the rules of this land. He's working by the rules of love. And we are His.

SEE ::

Watch video Session 5: **WORTHLESS**.

Use streaming instructions on inside cover or DVD.

Take notes if you like.

ASK ::

Use Session 5: **WORTHLESS** Conversation Cards for group discussion.

Complete the STUDY and PROJECTS for Session 6: **TRUTH** before your next group meeting.

SESSION 6

TRUTH

Work through pages 148–173 on your own before your next group meeting and video teaching.

GUIDED PRAYER: BREATHE

Before we do anything today, I want you to stop. Take a deep breath. Inhale, exhale.

The very act of breathing is an invitation to connect with God. The word for God's name in Hebrew—YHWH—is the sound of your breath. You breathe in and breathe out, and in that moment, you are in the presence of God.

This isn't just metaphorical. It's real. In Romans 8, we're told that God's Word is right here, as close as the breath in your lungs.

"And if the Spirit of him who raised Jesus from the dead is living in you, he who raised Christ from the dead will also give life to your mortal bodies because of his Spirit who lives in you" (v. 11 NIV).

So, take a minute.

Breathe in, breathe out, and let that truth sink in:

God is near.
He's with you in this.

Now that you've breathed, invite the Holy Spirit to fill you. Stop and ask for it. Don't overthink it. Ephesians 5:18 says, "Be filled with the Spirit." Not a little bit filled—totally, completely, all the way filled.

Relax, and let the Spirit saturate every part of you. Don't resist. Don't quench the Spirit, which just means keeping Him from doing what He wants to do. Let Him do His work. As you let go and surrender, you'll feel peace that doesn't come from anywhere else. You'll begin to hear the still small voice of truth. That's the Holy Spirit at work in you.

GUIDED PRAYER: SEARCH

You've breathed, you've asked for the Spirit to fill you. Now it's time to connect.

Ask God to bind your heart, your mind, and your spirit to His. Everything you've been holding on to—the lies, the hurt, the false beliefs—you've got to let those things go. You've got to choose to be aligned with God. Matthew 18:18 tells us that we have the authority to bind and loose:

"'Whatever you bind on earth will be bound in heaven, and whatever you loose on earth will be loosed in heaven'" (NIV).

So, take that authority and bind yourself to God's Truth. Then, as James 4:7 says, "Resist the devil, and he will flee from you."

This is how you start the process of undoing the lies.

This is how you begin to walk in truth.

You know those lies you've been believing? It's time to get honest. Ask God to search you, to reveal to you every lie you've accepted as truth. Psalm 139:23–24 says:

"Search me, God, and know my heart;
test me and know my anxious thoughts.
See if there is any offensive way in me,
and lead me in the way everlasting" (NIV).

You can't fix something you aren't willing to face. So, let God show you those things.

There's no shame here. It's just you telling the truth about what you've been carrying. This is where the rubber hits the road and we accept the offer to step into the Light.

HAND IT OVER

Now, take the piece of paper with your lie on it, and imagine yourself giving it to Jesus. Imagine Him standing in front of you. Not as a distant figure but as a real person who loves you. Picture yourself handing that list over to Him. (Place the lie in a basket in the center of your group.)

- *What does He do with it?*
- *Does He take it and rip it up?*
- *Does He just look at you with compassion?*
- *Whatever He does, write that thing down.*

____

____

____

This is the moment of exchange. You're handing over the lies. You're letting Jesus take what you've believed about yourself, and in return, He's going to give you something better. Something true.

> "At that time the disciples came to Jesus, saying, 'Who is the greatest in the kingdom of heaven?' And calling to him a child, he put him in the midst of them and said, 'Truly, I say to you, unless you turn and become like children, you will never enter the kingdom of heaven'" (Matthew 18:1–3).

CREATED TO BE GOD'S CHILD

Throughout this study, we've talked about our childhood memories. The ones that stick with us as the moments we first started believing the lies *I'm helpless, I'm unlovable, I'm worthless,* when the enemy began whispering in our ears. I don't think that's what Jesus is talking about when He's describing the humility of a child. He's describing their baseline state.

What are kids like?

They're messy. (Very messy.) They're joyous. They're exuberant. Creative. They're full of the adventure of what life could be. They cry. They belly laugh. They mess up. They don't do things the "right" way, but we melt a little when we watch them trying. They fall and get hurt. And they come running to their parents to make it all better.

That's my heart for this process. That it makes us like the kid versions of ourselves, before the enemy started to leak lies into our ears. Free. Creative. And running to our Father. Running out of the Dark and into His presence.

The final part of our time together is to prepare you to turn back to the Kingdom of Light, again and again. How to remember your identity as a child of God who walks where lies don't win. This whole journey isn't just about naming lies. It's about *living your life in truth* every day.

STUDY ::

Read Matthew 18:1–3.

RESPOND

How does Jesus describe the process of "turning" here?

What do you think the disciples were turning against? Turning toward?

What is required to enter His kingdom?

What does it mean to humble yourself like a child?

Read Revelation 22:1–5.

Envision that free version of you as a child, leaving the Dark, walking into this Kingdom of Light. How would she behave there? What would she do?

In light of this verse and what you now know, what are the first five words that come to mind when describing the Light Kingdom?

Where does the light come from?

What is not there? What do you not need?

"There will be no more night. They will not need the light of a lamp or the light of the sun, for the Lord God will give them light. And they will reign for ever and ever" (Revelation 22:5 NIV).

One day, we'll live fully in God's kingdom, where nobody needs a lamp to light the way. We'll be with Him, fully nourished, fully home.

Until then, though, we're in a battle. It's dark out here. Satan's agenda is in full swing here. We're living on earth, where the Prince of this world reigns, and we need a lamp. We need to turn from one kingdom to another again and again.

So, I want to leave you with three points of light to guide you. When things get dark (and they will), when the lies that saturate the air you breathe start to pull you back (and they will), here's where to find a spark of light. I'm going to give you:

1. A ***PICTURE*** of the kingdom.

2. A ***POSTURE*** to walk forward in.

3. A ***PRACTICE*** to carry you through the day to day.

PICTURE

In this world, you are being lied to. That's a fact. But you can fight this by being able to formulate a picture in your mind of what is true. What the Light Kingdom is. That will help you never go back to that state of darkness, where you just didn't know what the devil's tactics were, or where they came from, or what they were doing to you. Where you didn't know what his kingdom looked and felt like. When the Dark creeps up on you, when everything feels hard, when real suffering is wearing you out, you can know:

This is not the end of the story.

You are not alone.

You belong to the Light.

That eternal perspective demolishes the Darkness. This was why, in every temptation we've covered from Matthew 4, those taunts bounced right off Jesus.

Take what You can, and You can get control. You won't be helpless . . .

"Jesus declared, 'I am the bread of life. Whoever comes to me will never go hungry, and whoever believes in me will never be thirsty'" (John 6:35 NIV).

If God really loved You, He'd be helping You. Test, so everyone can see . . .

"Neither death nor life, neither angels nor demons, neither the present nor the future, nor any powers, neither height nor depth, nor anything else in all creation, will be able to separate us from the love of God that is in Christ Jesus our Lord" (Romans 8:38–39 NIV).

If only You could be great and awesome, You could get the love You crave . . .

"[Jesus said,] 'Whoever wants to save their life will lose it, but whoever loses their life for me will find it'" (Matthew 16:25 NIV).

Picture God's kingdom. Things are upside down here. We picture and understand it more, and turn toward it, a little every day.

POSTURE

Let's build a posture to walk forward in.

How would your posture look if you were around someone who clearly hated you and was hostile toward you? You'd be tense, maybe curled in on yourself. Over time, I bet that hate would be visible on you—in your walk, in your bearing. That's what years of living in the enemy's lies can do to you.

Now, imagine your body being around someone who loved you, liked and treasured you, was committed to helping you.

You'd be upright. Loose and relaxed. Joyful.

When we live each day as God's kids, it does marvels to our confidence. We live with our shoulders up, our chins up, and our palms up. Ready to take what the world gives because He is holding us up. The posture of freedom is with-ness: with God.

This posture isn't just for when everything is going great. It's for the hard times. When you're tired, in pain, and your sight is darkened—the lies seem real. In that posture, you're ready to lean on Him. In the hard times, He's training the muscles that hold you up. You turn to Him again and again. You build those muscles a little every day. Through endurance, resilience, long-suffering, and overcoming. And through it all, God is with you. He is the God who walks with you, close beside you, holding your hand, strengthening you, delighting in you.

LOCATE

For each of the verses below, make notes about your observations in the three columns.

SCRIPTURE	WHERE GOD IS	WHERE I AM	WHAT IS MY POSTURE? HOW DOES THIS STRENGTHEN ME GOING FORWARD?
Psalm 23:4			
Isaiah 41:10			
Psalm 46:1			
Psalm 34:18			
Isaiah 43:2			
Psalm 37:23–24			
1 Peter 5:7			

PRACTICE

"We are citizens of heaven, where the Lord Jesus Christ lives. And we are eagerly waiting for him to return as our Savior" (Philippians 3:20 NLT).

If we're citizens of heaven, what do citizens do? What are their ways? What are their practices? That's what I mean by *practice* here. Heaven's practices are ours.

Practices aren't just habits; they help us soak up every holy moment in the place we are in. Every day, we get to inhabit this new kingdom. And when we participate in the Light Kingdom, our practices help us name, release, and replace our lies with what is lovely, pure, and noble. We practice taking action, and in those little actions, we turn a little every day.

Let's talk about some *real-life* practices you can start right now. And I'm not kidding: They are practical practices.

Because yes—God is the Healer, the Rescuer, the Truth-teller—but sometimes we also need to *go to therapy and drink a glass of water.* You know what I mean? Here are some ideas.

- ***Get therapy.*** Sitting down with a wise, trained voice who can help you work through the lies from your story? Game changer. There's zero shame in needing help to reframe the junk we've been carrying around for years.

- ***Speak truth from Scripture.*** Jesus fought the devil with Scripture. You can too. Speak God's Word out loud. Into the mirror if you have to. Write it on your bathroom walls. Replace the voice of the enemy with statements that anchor you in the Truth of God.

- ***Know that stillness is not weakness.*** Mindfulness, silence, meditation—these are holy practices. They quiet the noise so we can hear what's true.

- ***Move your body.*** Exercise isn't just about health—it reminds you that you're alive, that you're strong. It can lift the fog and help you feel whole again.

- ***Learn something new every day.*** Pick up a book. Take a course. The more you learn, the more your confidence grows.

- ***Practice gratitude.*** This one flips everything. Even on the hardest days, look for something—anything—to thank God for. Gratitude shifts your soul.

- And last—but not even close to least—***Put your trust in a God who sees it all, knows it all, and still calls you loved.*** Because He's not asking you to fix yourself. He's asking you to follow Him.

As you walk through your days, you'll have so many tiny opportunities to choose which customs to practice. Sometimes you'll be pushed by pain, one way or the other. The Darkness may promise escape, but in the Light, you'll grow as you go. You'll get stronger. And it *will* get less painful—but not because life gets easier. Because you've become at home in the Kingdom of Light.

How can you "picture" the Kingdom of Light a little more every day?

How can you build a "posture" of walking with God a little more every day?

When can you commit to "locating" direction and confidence through daily reading of God's Word?

How can you "practice" what's good and true a little more every day?

WHO ARE YOU, LORD? & WHAT DO YOU WANT FROM ME?

Read: Romans 12:2. In light of what you read, answer the questions above.

DIGGING DEEPER

(OPTIONAL PROJECT FOR THOSE OF YOU WANTING TO GO DEEPER)

Dig deeper into:

- John 6:35

  What does this verse have to say to those who feel helpless?

- Romans 8:38–39

  What do these verses have to say to those who feel unlovable?

- Matthew 16:26

  What does this verse have to say to those who feel worthless?

PROJECT 1

PICTURE

Picture the two kingdoms. Sketch out what the Dark Kingdom has looked like for you on the left. Then envision what living in the Light Kingdom will look like going forward, and draw it on the right. (If you're not a draw-er, you can describe or choose a collection of words.)

DARK KINGDOM	LIGHT KINGDOM
The lies flatten you.	The picture of the Kingdom lifts your eyes (Isaiah 40:26).

DARK KINGDOM	LIGHT KINGDOM
The lies isolate you.	The picture of the Kingdom calls you into mission (1 Peter 2:9).

DARK KINGDOM	LIGHT KINGDOM
The lies name you by your pain.	The picture of the Kingdom names you by your inheritance (Romans 8:16–17).

▸ *How do these pictures give you confidence? How do they prepare you?*

PROJECT 2

POSTURE

In Joshua 4, God directs Joshua to set up "stones of remembrance" to mark the Israelites' miraculous crossing over the Jordan River. Any time their children would wonder, "What are those rocks about?" they'd tell the story of their powerful God, who walked with them, loved them, and delivered them.

Make your own stone of remembrance.

- *Choose a verse from the LOCATE section on page 159 that really speaks to you about the posture God has toward you and you have toward Him.*
- *Find a smooth, pocket-size stone, and write or paint your verse on it. (Or just designate it your reminder to call the verse to mind.)*
- *Slip it in your pocket this week. Every time you touch it, remember what it means about your powerful God, who walks with you. And stand up a little taller. Breathe a little freer because of who you are with.*
- *How does this change your posture, inside and out?*

PROJECT 3

PRACTICE

Practice is our way of walking in the ways of Light, while we're still in this life. While the Kingdom of Light is here now, it's also "not yet" as our final home where we will be with God forever.

When you feel yourself breathing Dark-Kingdom atmosphere, you can practice turning to the Light in small ways. Like these:

DARK KINGDOM LIFE	LIGHT KINGDOM LIFE	RIGHT-NOW PRACTICE (IN-BETWEEN MOMENTS)
Exhaustion	Eternal rest	A quiet nap, deep breath, Sabbath space
Judgment	Full acceptance	Being known and not rejected
Striving	Peace	A moment of stillness in prayer
Disorientation	Belonging	Being welcomed into a home or room
Rejection	Unconditional love	A friend's kind word at the right time
Limitations	Resurrection hope	Laughter in suffering
Hiding	Seen and celebrated	Eye contact that says, "I see you"
Lost in the dark	Flooded with light	Morning sun through the window
Scarcity	Abundance	A surprise meal or act of kindness
Death	Life that never ends	Singing when you shouldn't be able to

Write about what practices you need in your life most right now.

PROJECT 4

REFLECT

In light of everything you have learned in this study, what are you leaving behind?

What are you moving toward?

CONCLUSION

Listen, even as I type these words, I still have times I am hit with my core lie. I wish I could send you off with complete freedom. But here is what is completely different for me and I hope for you . . . I know where these thoughts come from and I know God is with me to fight back.

And now I *name the lie, fight it, drag it into the light, and beat it down with a stick in Jesus' name.*

I don't do passive faith. I'm more like: *Let's go find the root of this junk and rip it out.*

So, I fight to believe the truth that kills my lie. I fight to believe I'm seen and loved. I fight to remember I'm delighted in. And God? He meets me in that fight. He doesn't shame me for being back in the fight again. He just grabs the other end of the stick and helps me swing.

Because the truth is: I *am* seen. I *am* safe. I *am* loved. And so are you.

Even on the days when you feel like a mess.

We can't talk our way out of these lies. We can't think our way out. Or know enough Bible verses to Bible our way out. And as much as you'd like to, you can't beat it out. Because this isn't just about doing things differently.

It's about switching kingdoms—again and again. Going from Dark to Light. It's about holding onto your identity as a citizen of the Kingdom of Light, and turning toward it, a little more every day.

The enemy is never going to shut his mouth. He will always be whispering to you that if you can just fix it, or achieve it, or control it, you'll feel better. That your deepest wounds will be eased. Of course, our hearts want to believe that. But he's a liar.

The kingdom of God is a whole different way. He is a good King with all different rules. The world requires performance, control, and approval. All God asks of you is that you choose to walk with Him.

Say yes to His kingdom.

Fight the lie with the truth from the God who adores you.

SEE ::

Watch video Session 6: **TRUTH**.

Use streaming instructions on inside cover or DVD.

Take notes if you like.

ASK ::

Use Session 6: **TRUTH** Conversation Cards for group discussion.

LEADER'S GUIDE

Dear leader,

I am grateful for the chance to equip you in your efforts to disciple others! I pray that these few short pages will help to prepare you to lead this study. You may have led plenty of groups in the past, or perhaps this is the first one. Whichever is the case, this is a spiritual calling, and you are entering spiritual places with these participants—and spiritual callings and places need spiritual power.

My husband, Zac, always says, "Changed lives change lives." If you are not first aware of your own need for life change, the people around you won't see their need. If you allow God into the inner struggles of your heart, the people following you will be much more likely to let Him into theirs. Thank you for leading the way.

I've learned that the environment we live in tells us a lot of untrue things about ourselves. Living in this world, we start to believe lies. And we don't even know it. How do we combat these lies? Not just by telling the truth instead. It will take a change of the kind only Jesus can give to walk in the Light.

This study is my invitation for you to hold your most vulnerable moments and most deeply ingrained lies up to the Light. To allow your mind and heart and body to adjust to living in God's kingdom, instead of in a place where lies are the law of the land. So, the lies just fall away.

Through these six weeks together, we'll learn that when we are bold enough to uncover the lies we don't know we believe, Jesus has a land of freedom and truth, of lightness and confidence, waiting for us.

This journey invites us to name our core lie, discover where it came from, and find out what God has to say about and to us as we embrace healing and freedom. I want a life where, instead of existing with that sense of unease we can't put our finger on, we wake up. We notice the lies in the air we breathe, name them, and let God change our perspective. We'll see how Jesus did this as He directly confronted Satan's lies in the book of Matthew. We can fight like He did.

Together, we can do this. We can and we will encourage one another, hold each other accountable, and fix our eyes on Jesus. That is where we will find true freedom. God made us to walk in grace and in truth. Let's take a bold step together toward the freedom we were meant for.

Grateful,

Jennie

PREPARING YOURSELF TO LEAD

1. Pray

Pray for yourself: Pray that you would be led by the Spirit. Pray that you would lead with wisdom, compassion, discernment, and urgency. Pray fervently and continuously.

Pray for your study participants that they would:

- embrace God's Truth and feel safe to open up and connect.
- have hearts that are teachable and moldable.
- be transformed by God's Word and His Spirit.

2. Lean on God

Don't lead this Bible study in your own power. Allow the Holy Spirit to lead every moment—your preparation, your facilitation, your follow-up.

Don't just teach what's on the page. Allow the Spirit freedom to work outside the boundaries of your plan and agenda.

Depend on God for the results. Don't try to manufacture moments or experiences. Keep in mind your responsibility is to be obedient and faithful to teach the Word. The results are left to God.

Teach out of the overflow of your own walk with God. You can't pour out much truth from an empty pitcher. Spend time daily with the Savior in an intimate love relationship with Him. Let Him pour into you before you pour out on others.

3. Be Vulnerable

There will be times you will need to open up and share your life. This will help others feel safe to share. But don't feel like you have to share every detail. You don't. Share what is necessary, guided by the Holy Spirit.

4. Listen, but Also Lead

Allow people to share their struggles and do your best not to interrupt. However, you will need to guide the conversation. Include everyone in the discussion. You may need to continue to steer the conversation back to the truth of God's Word.

5. Model Trust

Don't be a "do as I say" leader. Be the example. Apply what you have learned and are learning through the study.

THE STUDY: SESSION TOOLS AND FORMAT

The Lie You Don't Know You Believe is designed to work in various types of venues and locations, including homes, dorm rooms, workplaces, and churches. Whether you find yourself leading a large group of people at church or a few neighbors in your home, the study is intended for small groups to share and process truth. I suggest a maximum number of eight people in your group. If you are leading a large group at church, divide into smaller groups and enlist people to lead each small group.

WHAT A LEADER NEEDS

Study Guide. Each study guide comes with this leader's guide and streaming video access.

Conversation Card Deck. Each deck includes group discussion questions and a memory verse card for each session.

SESSION TOOLS AND HOW TO USE THEM

STUDY

Every participant will need a Bible study guide. Distribute the books at your first group meeting and walk participants through them. Point out the weekly Study section, followed by the Projects. These can be completed in one sitting or spaced throughout the week. The lessons in the book (except for the first lesson) should be completed between group meetings.

The lessons are interactive, designed to help people study Scripture for themselves and apply it to their lives. The Projects in the Bible study guide will provide creative options for applying Scripture. Some of these experiences may push participants outside their comfort zones. Encourage them to be brave and tackle the challenge. Make sure to discuss the Projects at each group meeting.

SEE

Open each group gathering by reviewing the Study and Projects experiences from the previous week and asking if anyone had anything specific to share or ask about. Watch the short, engaging video teaching to introduce the lesson, set the tone for your time together, and challenge your group to apply Scripture. If your group members want to take notes, encourage them to use the Notes page opposite each SEE title page. Each study guide includes instructions for personal access to the streaming videos on the inside front cover. This is perfect for anyone who might miss a group gathering, wants to rewatch any of the video teaching, or if your group needs to meet on shortened time.

ASK

After the video teaching is complete, ask the group if anything in particular stood out while you prepare the Conversation Cards. The Conversation Cards provide a unique way to jump-start honest discussion. Each week's cards are labeled with the appropriate lesson title and can be used after the video or teaching time. The following is a suggested step-by-step way to use the cards.

- Begin by laying out the Scripture Cards for that specific week.
- Direct each group member to take a card.
- Go over the Ground Rules each week. (Ground Rules are found on page 186 and on the back of the Instruction card.)
- Take turns presenting the question on each card to the group. Provide adequate time for everyone in your group to respond to each question.

Don't feel pressured to read and answer every card. Be sensitive to the leading of the Holy Spirit and your time constraints. Remind the group that what they share and how they share are entirely personal decisions. No one should be forced to answer every card.

NOTE:

Make use of this leader's guide to facilitate a great Bible study experience for your group. It will help you point people to the overarching theme for each lesson and give you specific suggestions on how to share the truth and foster discussion.

SESSION FORMAT

This six-session study is designed to go deep very quickly, so it's flexible when considering the length of your group sessions. It can be led in a church spread out over a couple of hours, or in a break room over a one-hour lunch. However, the more time you can allow for discussion, the better. When the group is given deep questions and space to reflect and respond, you'll be surprised by the depth and beauty of the conversations.

You will be the best judge of what time and format works for your group. However, here is a suggested schedule for each group meeting.

1. **OPEN—Personal study discussion (15–35 minutes)**

   After a warm welcome and opening prayer, provide time for the group to share and discuss their personal reflections from the Study of Scripture and the Projects.

   If you have more than eight in your group, break into smaller groups for this discussion.

2. **SEE—Video teaching (17–18 minutes)**

   Use the video to lay the foundation for the week's lesson and transition to the Conversation Cards. Feel free to provide supplemental teaching for your group.

3. **ASK—Conversation Cards (25–75 minutes)**

   Allow time for each group member to ask and discuss the question on each card. If you need an extra set of cards, they are available for purchase from your favorite online retailer.

4. **CLOSE—Closing (5–10 minutes)**

   Pray as a group and encourage everyone to engage in the Study before meeting again.

   Always encourage the group members to abide by the following Ground Rules for discussion. These rules can be found on the next page, on the back of the Instruction card, and on page 6 of this Bible study book.

GROUND RULES

BE CONCISE.

Share your answers to the questions while protecting others' time for sharing. Be considerate. Don't be afraid to share with the group but try not to dominate the conversation.

KEEP GROUP MEMBERS' STORIES CONFIDENTIAL.

Your group members will want to share sensitive and personal information with you, not with your husband or other friends. Protect each other by not allowing anything shared in the group to leave the group.

RELY ON SCRIPTURE FOR TRUTH.

Conventional, worldly wisdom has value, but it is not absolute truth. Only Scripture provides that. In your times of discussion, be careful not to equate good advice with God's truth.

NO COUNSELING.

Work together to protect the group by not directing all attention toward solving one person's problem. This is the place for confession and discovery and applying truth together as a group. However, at times a member may need to dig even deeper with an outside counselor or talk with a friend outside of small group time. If that is you, don't be afraid to ask for help, or be sure and follow up with a member of the group.

WHEN TO REFER

Some of the people in your group may be dealing with issues beyond your ability to help. If you sense that someone may need more extensive help, refer them to speak with your pastor or a trained Christian counselor. Maintain the relationship and follow up with them to make sure they are getting the care needed. You or someone else in your group may need to walk with them through this season of their life. As we have said many times, be sensitive to the Holy Spirit's leading as you love and offer hope to the people in your group.

TYPES OF LEARNERS

Hopefully, you will be blessed to be leading this study with a group diverse in age, experience, and style. While the benefits of coming together as a diverse group to discuss God outweigh the challenges by a mile, there are often distinctions in learning styles. Just be aware and consider some of the differences that may be represented. (These are obviously generalizations, and each person will express his or her own unique communication style, but in general these are common characteristics.)

EXPERIENTIAL LEARNERS

These are women who are more transparent, don't like anything cheesy, want to go deep quickly, and are passionate. Make a safe environment for them by being transparent yourself and engaging their hearts. These women may not care as much about head knowledge and may care more deeply how knowledge about God applies to their lives. They want to avoid being put in a box. Keep the focus on applying truth to their lives and they will stay engaged. Don't preach to them; be real and show them through your experiences how to pursue the mind of Christ.

PRAGMATIC LEARNERS

These women are more accustomed to a traditional, inductive, or precept approach to Bible study. They have a high value for truth and authority but may not place as high a value on the emotional aspects of confessing sin and being vulnerable. To them it may feel unnecessary or dramatic. Keep the focus on the truth of Scripture. These women keep truth in the forefront of their lives and play a valuable role in discipleship.

Because this study is different from traditional studies, some women may need more time to get used to the approach. The goal is still to make God big in our lives, to fix our minds on Him, and to choose to walk in His Truth over lies. We all just approach it in unique ways to reach unique types of people. I actually wrote this study praying it could reach both types of learners. I am one who lives with a foot in both worlds, trying to apply the deep truths I gained in seminary in an experiential way. I pray that this study would deeply engage the heart and the mind, and that we would be people who worship God in spirit and in truth, not just learning about the battle for our lives but going to war for them together.

SESSION 1

IDENTIFY

Note to leader: The teaching format for this session is different from the other sessions because it is the first group time and there is no personal study to review. Participants are encouraged to complete the session material and Project on pages 10–23 on their own to acclimate to the purpose of this study. These pages can be done after viewing and discussing the video or on their own time.

1. **OPEN**

   Welcome the participants to your group and take a few moments for introductions. Briefly share about yourself and allow others to do the same. After introductions, lead the group in prayer.

   Distribute the Bible study guides to group members and go over the Instructions and Expectations on pages 4–8. Explain that they have individual access to the streaming videos so everyone can keep up with the study, regardless of an unavoidable missed gathering.

2. **SEE**

   View Session 1 video: IDENTIFY.

3. **ASK**

   Transition to the Conversation Cards for discussion. The cards for this week are labeled "Session 1—IDENTIFY" on the front. Lead participants to choose, answer, and discuss the questions on the cards. (You can review the instructions for using the cards in "SESSION FORMAT" on page 185.)

4. CLOSE

Close by asking the group to write down three things:

- One thing they learned from this session
- One reason they are excited about this study
- One question they have moving forward

Briefly discuss their responses. Do so with little or no commentary but pay close attention to the answers. If time allows, close by praying specifically for each person in your group, using one of each person's responses as the focus of your prayer for them.

Read this week's Scripture memory verse aloud to the group and tell the group to commit each verse to memory as best they can.

"But when anything is exposed by the light, it becomes visible, for anything that becomes visible is light" (Ephesians 5:13–14).

Instruct the group to complete Session 2 Study and Projects before the next group meeting.

SESSION 2

KINGDOMS

MAIN IDEA: *Moving from deeply ingrained lies to truth is about more than just trying harder or believing the truth. It requires walking out of one kingdom and into another. The enemy holds sway over this world, what we'll call the Kingdom of Darkness, and lies are the law here. But God's kingdom, the Kingdom of Light,* *reveals the truth. It's our true home, and we can walk into it any time we want. Now that we've identified and spotted our lies, we'll learn what it means to live in these kingdoms. How can we notice when we're living in the Dark? How can we choose to live in the Light? What's the difference?*

In this session we will look at the reality of the spiritual battle going on all around us. We will intentionally pay attention to enemy tactics and what he is up to in the lives of those who love God. We will learn how to identify the broken reality around us, and learn about the reality God created us to exist in. We'll learn to claim God's kingdom as our own and what that means for the lies we believe about ourselves.

Here are some general goals and thoughts for your time together this week.

- Identify and define the nature of the Dark Kingdom surrounding us.
- Discover the attributes of the Light Kingdom that invite us to walk in freedom from that Darkness.
- Discuss the ways God invites us to be set free and choose His kingdom instead.

MAIN GOAL: *Lead people to a frank assessment of the spiritual state of this world—that we are not on neutral ground—and familiarize them with the choice we have to walk from one world to another: God's Kingdom of Light.*

1. OPEN

Begin by reviewing the personal study and Projects from last week. Here are some suggested places to focus on as you review:

- What truth stood out to you about the Dark Kingdom? What about the Light?
- How does Ephesians 6:11–12 blow open our everyday perceptions of this world? Why is it so easy to forget this?
- Share your experiences with Project 2: Walk on New Ground.
- What else stood out to you from the lesson and Scripture that you want to learn more about, find hope in, and/or apply?

2. **SEE**

Watch Session 2 video: KINGDOMS.

3. **ASK**

Transition to the Conversation Cards to continue your discussion. The cards for this week are labeled "Session 2—KINGDOMS" on the front. Lead the group to choose, answer, and discuss the questions on the cards. (You can review the instructions for using the cards in "SESSION FORMAT" on page 185.)

4. **CLOSE**

Ask: "What is one thing you noticed in your everyday life that points to the fact that we don't live in a neutral world? How has that informed the lies you've believed?" Encourage group members to choose a partner and share their answers to that question with each other. Then challenge them to pray for each other.

Read this week's Scripture memory verse aloud to the group and tell the group to commit each verse to memory as best they can.

"The night is nearly over; the day is almost here. So let us put aside the deeds of darkness and put on the armor of light" (Romans 13:12).

Encourage the group to complete Session 3 Study and Projects before the next group meeting.

SESSION 3

HELPLESS

MAIN IDEA: *There are three main lies we will focus on together. Most of us believe at least one of them. So, we'll dig into all three. First, we'll explore the lie I'm helpless, and discover how the enemy uses it to get to us and what he hopes it will do to us. We'll witness Jesus combatting this lie in Matthew 4, and we'll dig into how we can embrace this truth for ourselves as we learn to live in His reality, rather than the lie.*

Here are some general goals and thoughts for your time together this week.

- Explore where the belief *I'm helpless* might have come from and confront it with compassion in our own childhood selves.
- Gain clarity on how the lie affects our behaviors and reactions now.
- Remember what God is like, and how He gives us spiritual authority to confront lies.

MAIN GOAL: *Learn to exercise spiritual authority instead of believing the lie* I'm helpless. *Help people recognize enemy tactics and remind them that they are helped by the Helper. Remember that surrendering to Jesus makes us stronger.*

1. OPEN

Begin by reviewing the personal study and Projects from last week. Here are some suggested places to focus on as you review:

- Discuss the story of Jesus confronting Satan in Matthew 4. What can we learn about Jesus' spiritual authority from this story?

- Do you see a way that the lie *I'm helpless* has shown up in the way you live today?
- What stood out to you in Matthew 18:18–20?
- Have the group share their Fighter verse from Project 4.
- What else stood out to you from the lesson and Scripture that you need to learn, treasure, and/or apply?

2. SEE

Watch Session 3 video: HELPLESS.

3. ASK

Transition to the Conversation Cards to continue your discussion. The cards for this week are labeled "Session 3—HELPLESS" on the front. Lead the group to choose, answer, and discuss the questions on the cards. (You can review the instructions for using the cards in "SESSION FORMAT" on page 185.)

4. CLOSE

Invite the group to look at the chart in Project 1 and share a word that best describes how the enemy is making them feel, and what accusations that translates to for them. Pray for the person to your right after they share.

Read this week's Scripture memory verse aloud to the group and tell the group to commit each verse to memory as best they can.

"When the Spirit of truth comes, he will guide you into all the truth, for he will not speak on his own authority, but whatever he hears he will speak, and he will declare to you what is to come" (John 16:13).

Close with prayer.

Encourage the group to complete Session 4 Study and Projects before the next group meeting.

SESSION 4

UNLOVABLE

MAIN IDEA: *Somewhere in our past, many of us have latched on to the lie* I'm unlovable. *We looked all around us, and we seemed to see proof everywhere we looked. Satan hopes to convince us that if God really loved us the way we were, He would be doing things differently. So, God must not love us. But knowing who God is, is the best way to fight a lie. And in this case, we can know the truth that God not only loves us, but He* likes *us. And that changes everything.*

Here are some general goals and thoughts for your time together this session.

- Help the group see the way the enemy tries to use "proof" to convince us of lies.
- Explore the way the enemy might be using unmet desires and disappointments to speak lies to us.

- Remember together that the best way to fight a lie is to remember who God is, and what life is like in the land where He reigns.
- Let the fact that God likes us change our posture toward Him.

MAIN GOAL: *Lead people to call out the lie* I'm unlovable, *identify the enemy's tactics, and overwhelm those tactics with God's presence and His nature as Love itself.*

1. OPEN

Begin by reviewing the personal study and Projects from last week.

Here are some suggested places to focus on as you review:

- Reflect on the verses in the section "God Likes You." Do you believe them?
- What did you feel as you read the story of Jesus shutting down the devil in Matthew 4? What does "Do not put . . . God to the test" mean (v. 7 NIV)?
- Which Project stood out to you most this session?
- What else stood out to you from the lesson and Scripture that you need to learn, treasure, and/or apply?

2. SEE

Watch session 4 video: UNLOVABLE.

3. ASK

Transition to the Conversation Cards to continue your discussion. The cards for this week are labeled "Session 4—UNLOVABLE" on the front. Lead the group to choose, answer, and discuss the questions on the cards. (You can review the instructions for using the cards in "SESSION FORMAT" on page 185.)

4. CLOSE

Close by sharing a personal story about how it has made a difference in you to be openly liked versus disliked or just tolerated, and how it affects you to truly believe that God not only loves but likes you. Ask if any group member is going through a tough time right now in feeling unlovable. If one or more people indicate this is true in their lives, circle around them and pray for them.

Read this week's Scripture memory verse aloud to the group and tell the group to commit each verse to memory as best they can.

"'The LORD your God is in your midst, a mighty one who will save; he will rejoice over you with gladness; he will quiet you by his love; he will exult over you with loud singing'" (Zephaniah 3:17).

Encourage the group to complete Session 5 Study and Projects before the next group meeting.

SESSION 5

WORTHLESS

MAIN IDEA: *The lie* I'm worthless *often shows up in our need to achieve and be awesome. The enemy whispers to us that we'd better do more and work harder to avoid being a disappointment. But Jesus shows us that in His world, we play by* *different rules. We can fail, and it even brings us closer to God. We don't have to perform. We don't have to be "enough." Because He is "enough" for us.*

Here are some general goals and thoughts for your time together this session.

- Connect all that we've learned in noticing and naming the lies we believe and what it means to call them out and put words to them.
- Discover how our drive to hit marks or be "splendid" shows up in our lives, and how that might be connected to the lie *I'm worthless*.
- Notice the way that lie operates as truth in the Dark Kingdom, and what the difference is in the Light Kingdom.
- Start to make friends with failure and let it all lead us back to worship.
- Learn the difference between "worthless" and "not enough."

MAIN GOAL: *Encourage people to expose the lie* I'm worthless *and the ways it may be operating in their motivations and choices. Then discover how who God is takes the pressure off us to perform and prove ourselves worthy and instead leads us to worship a worthy God.*

1. OPEN

Begin by reviewing the personal study and Projects from last week. Here are some suggested places to focus on as you review.

- Talk about the kinds of things you might have on your scorecard. What would it mean to fail at one of those things?

- Discuss how the story of Jesus healing on the Sabbath shows the difference between the Dark Kingdom and the Light Kingdom. What happens to our box checking in the face of God's love?
- Discuss the barriers you face in admitting that you can be "not enough," and that can be okay?
- What stood out to you from the lesson and Scripture that you need to learn, treasure, and/or apply?

2. SEE

Watch session 5 video: WORTHLESS.

3. ASK

Transition to the Conversation Cards to continue your discussion. The cards for this week are labeled "Session 5—WORTHLESS" on the front. Lead the group to choose, answer, and discuss the questions on the cards. (You can review the instructions for using the cards in "SESSION FORMAT" on page 185.)

4. CLOSE

Challenge each member of your group to pray for surrender, such as, "Lord, show me where I can lay down striving and trust You in my fears of . . . ." Encourage them to write the prayer in their book or Bible and date it. Emphasize that this is not a prayer to pray lightly. Provide a quiet moment for them to consider what it means to lay down these things, then close with prayer.

Read this week's Scripture memory verse aloud to the group and tell the group to commit each verse to memory as best they can.

> "But he said to me, 'My grace is sufficient for you, for my power is made perfect in weakness'" (2 Corinthians 12:9).

Encourage the group to complete Session 6 Study and Projects before the next group meeting.

SESSION 6

TRUTH

MAIN IDEA: *Living in the light of God's Truth is a daily turning—a daily choice to turn away from our lie and toward the truth. We can be empowered and equipped to walk forward in the Light, so we're living fully in our identity as God's children—and living in an environment where lies fall off us.*

Here are some general goals and thoughts for your time together this session.

- Turning from lies to truth, from Darkness to Light, is more than a one-time deal; it's a daily practice.
- Focus on the long view. This is a process we will have to repeat moment by moment, and we'll need to hold onto our Father like a child.
- If you don't know what to do, discuss what you need with the group and be brave enough to ask for help.
- God gave us tools to stay in the Light: a picture of the Kingdom, a posture to stand and walk in every day, and practices that support our daily turning toward Him.

MAIN GOAL: *Explore next steps in this process of living as a native in the Kingdom of Light.*

1. **OPEN**

Begin by reviewing the personal study and Projects from last week. Here are some suggested places to focus on as you review.

- Pray through the list of real-life practices with God to see if He leads you to know or do something that can lead you into a deeper and more fulfilling life in the Light Kingdom.
- Discuss verses on pageS 156–157 about the eternal perspective versus Satan's lie. What stands out to you about Jesus' view versus the earthly view?
- Share the answers to Project 4. What are you leaving behind and what are you moving toward?
- What will you keep from this week's session as a powerful reminder that your citizenship is in heaven?
- What else stood out to you from the lesson and Scripture that you need to learn, treasure, and/or apply?

2. **SEE**

Watch session 6 video: TRUTH.

3. **ASK**

Transition to the Conversation Cards to continue your discussion. The cards for this week are labeled "Session 6—TRUTH" on the front. Lead the group to choose, answer, and discuss the questions on the cards. (You can review the instructions for using the cards in "SESSION FORMAT" on page 185.)

4. CLOSE

Share a personal experience you've had in these weeks together. Allow the group to share similar stories. If a member of your group is having difficulty with anything that exploring their lies may have raised, or facing anxiety about it, take a moment to surround them and pray for them.

Read this week's Scripture memory verse aloud to the group and remind the group to go back through all the memory verses from weeks one through six. Encourage them to keep committing these verses to memory as they continue through these new practices of *untangling their emotions*—these verses will guide them and lead them well.

"We are citizens of heaven, where the Lord Jesus Christ lives. And we are eagerly waiting for him to return as our Savior" (Philippians 3:20 NLT).

HOW TO FIND GOD

If anyone in your group is unsure of her relationship with Jesus and feels led to give her life to Christ definitively, lead her through these basic tenets of faith.

Humanity had a perfect relationship with God until sin entered the world through Adam and Eve. With sin came the certainty of death and eternal separation from God. The penalty had to be paid. But at the same moment that He named the punishment for the first sin, God issued His promise to provide a way for us to return to Him.

Our sin was to be placed on the perfect sacrifice. God would send His own blameless, perfect Son to bear our sin and suffer our deserved fate—to get us back.

Jesus came, fulfilling thousands of years of prophecy, lived a perfect life, and died a gruesome death, satisfying the payment for our sin. Then after three days, He defeated death, rose from the grave, and is now seated with the Father.

Anyone who accepts the blood of Jesus for the forgiveness of their sins can be adopted as a child of God. To each one who believes, God issues His very own Spirit to seal and empower us to live this life for and with Him.

We were made for God, and He gave everything so that our souls could finally and forever find their rest in Him.

If you have never trusted Christ for the forgiveness of your sins, you can do that this moment. Just tell Him you need Him and tell Him you choose to trust Him as your Lord and Savior.

ABOUT THE AUTHOR

Jennie Allen is a Bible teacher, author, podcast host and visionary leader. As the founder of IF:Gathering and Gather25, a vision to mobilize the global Church, Jennie has devoted her life to disciple a generation to see revival across the globe.

Jennie has written three *New York Times* bestsellers, *Untangle Your Emotions*, *Find Your People*, and *Get Out of Your Head*, inspiring millions to experience freedom in Christ and connection with others.

Jennie holds a master's degree in Biblical Studies from Dallas Theological Seminary and lives in Dallas, Texas, with her husband, Zac, and their four children.

Connect with Jennie at www.jennieallen.com, on Instagram @jennieallen, or listen at *The Jennie Allen Podcast.*

ALSO AVAILABLE FROM JENNIE ALLEN

DISCOVER HOW GOD MADE YOU FEEL

In this seven-session video Bible study Jennie helps you discover that emotions that are submitted to God and used for the purposes God intends connect us to each other and to Him.

BUILDING DEEP COMMUNITY IN A LONELY WORLD

In this seven-session video Bible study, Jennie looks at the original community in Genesis, the Trinity, and the creation of people to see what God had planned for us all along offering practical solutions for creating true community in a world that's both more connected and more isolating than ever before.

STOPPING THE SPIRAL OF TOXIC THOUGHTS

In *Get Out of Your Head*, a six-session, video-based Bible study, Jennie inspires and equips us to transform our emotions, our outlooks, and even our circumstances by taking control of our thoughts.

YOU ARE ENOUGH BECAUSE JESUS IS ENOUGH.

In this eight-session study, Jennie Allen walks through key passages in the Gospel of John that demonstrate how Jesus is enough. We don't have to prove anything because Jesus has proven everything.

IDENTIFY THE THREADS OF YOUR LIFE

In this DVD-based study using the story of Joseph, Jennie explains how his suffering, gifts, story, and relationships fit into the greater story of God—and how your story can do the same.

THE PLACES WE GET STUCK & THE GOD WHO SETS US FREE

Stuck is an eight-session Bible study experience leading women through the invisible struggles that we fight and to the God who sets us free.

CHASING AFTER THE HEART OF GOD

Chase is a seven-session Bible study experience to discover the heart of God and what it is exactly He wants from us through major events in the life of David and the psalms.

Visit JennieAllen.com for more info. Available wherever books & Bibles are sold.